simple light

wisdom from a woman's heart

Kabbalah Publishing is a registered DBA of
Kabbalah Centre International, Inc.

For further information:

The Kabbalah Centre
155 E. 48th St., New York, NY 10017
1062 S. Robertson Blvd., Los Angeles, CA 90035

1.800.Kabbalah www.kabbalah.com

First Edition
February 2008
Printed in USA
ISBN10: 1-57189-593-0
ISBN13: 978-1-57189-593-6

Design: HL Design (Hyun Min Lee) www.hldesignco.com

simple

wisdom from a woman's heart

KAREN BERG

author of *God Wears Lipstick*

simple

introduction

When you meet my mom, Karen, you'll notice right away that she is a special woman. It's in her presence, her passion, her gift for taking the most complex ideas or situations and turning them into simple truths that anyone can understand and benefit from. According to Kabbalah, the Light is simple; it's the Ego that complicates things. This is why when we hear truth—wisdom that is free from the influence of Ego—it touches us as profoundly simple and universal.

This is Kabbalah—wisdom so simple and universal that it can be understood by everyone. Yet for centuries, Kabbalah was concealed from the masses and understood by only a select few—that is, until my mom entered the picture.

When my mother started studying Kabbalah with my father, Rav Berg, almost 40 years ago, she said, "If I can understand this ancient wisdom—and I am no great scholar—then the rest of the world can also understand it and use it to improve the quality of their own lives." Since then, it has been through Karen's pure and uncomplicated lens that the wisdom of Kabbalah has been made accessible and understandable to anyone who craves its wisdom.

By prying open the doors of Kabbalah, she has enriched the lives of an entire generation. It is due to her immense courage and historic efforts that today millions around the world are studying and reaping the benefits of Kabbalah in their lives.

Why has Karen made this her life's work? Because she believes, as I do, that nothing should prevent people from accessing the wisdom and blessings that the Creator intends for all of us. God wants nothing more than for us to experience His Light and to share this profound joy with others. And that's exactly what Karen herself does—she lives a life of deep joy and unending contribution.

Simple Light is a collection of Karen's most inspiring thoughts and meditations compiled from hundreds of lectures that she has given throughout the world over the last three years since the Rav experienced his stroke. Under such difficult circumstances, some people might have become bitter or stopped living altogether. But not Karen! My mother continues to live each day to its fullest by spending every waking moment meeting with people and supporting their growth. She is an example of all that we teach—that life and happiness is a decision. I am honored to share her wisdom and her *Simple Light* with you.

You may choose to read one thought a day or just open this book whenever you want to make your life feel a little less complicated. My mom's words always seem to have that effect, as you'll soon discover.

It would be impossible to thank Karen for all that she has done for her family, the Centre, and the consciousness of the planet. We simply can't thank her enough, but I hope that by my putting this book together, she will come to know how much she is loved and appreciated for the incredible woman that she is and the simple Light that she possesses.

Yehuda Berg

simple light

There is a spiritual electric current encircling the globe. That spiritual electricity is known as *immortality*. Why is this happening? This is happening because we are moving closer to a time when spirituality will become the norm—a time that has never before been experienced by humanity. In a few years, things that are now viewed as charlatan will be encouraged and accepted. Even now, people are growing increasingly connected.

However, as we move closer to this revelation of Light, we are beginning to experience more natural upheaval—more hurricanes, more floods, more extreme weather. Why? Because Satan, our Opponent, wants to prevent this revelation of Light, which makes this time a pivotal point in the history of humanity. That's why we must come together now to spread the message of unification. In a world where so much disharmony exists, only the cancer cell has proved immortal. But we are the lamps of the lighthouse of Creation and the bearers of the gene of immortality.

onsciousness is the essence of the entire Bible. The Bible is the Book of Consciousness. The Bible is also the Book of Certainty, and we must read it as such.

A man once dreamed that there was a treasure hidden in the garden of a palace far away. The man, whose name was David, traveled to the palace he had seen in his dream, but when he got there, the guards stationed at the gate prevented him from entering. He didn't know what to do. Finally, he decided to approach one of the guards and tell him about his dream. The guard said to him, "Wow! Just last night, I dreamed that someone named David would come to me and tell me that the treasure he sought was buried under his own house."

Isn't that the way things are in our own lives? Sometimes we travel such a long way along our path, only to realize in the end that all the answers and treasures we have been seeking have been right in front of us the entire time.

I t is important to know that we are usually not at the level we think we are. In fact, if we think we have "arrived" spiritually, we probably haven't. We should always be working on moving to the next level. To do that, however, we need to know where we are now and acknowledge the dirt in our Vessel today. This is hard work, and it doesn't come for free.

We don't want to look back on our lives and regret that we didn't do more. How many of us know that we could be doing more? The time will come when we will all look back and ask, "Did I do enough? Did I share my gifts? Was there a place where I could have done more?"

The *Zohar* says that the Gates of Prayer are open for us through the birds, for the birds are the ones that carry our messages up high into the Upper Worlds.

The greatest part of being human is our ability to look at one another with tolerance and love. To look at people with anything less is a tragedy. Even if we don't see eye to eye, we must maintain this kinship because this is what separates human beings from animals.

The *Desire to Receive* is very small in an angel. This is because angels remain close to the Light of the Creator, which makes it very difficult for them to perform negative actions. They've tasted the Light, and near the Light is where they want to stay.

Everything has both a positive and a negative aspect. The *Zohar* asks: "How can we judge anything to be bad if we can take from it a piece of beauty?" It doesn't matter how negative something appears to be; we can always turn it into something beautiful.

Oftentimes, it's easier for someone who is new to the spiritual path to transform than it is for people who have been doing this work for a longer time. When we consider ourselves "spiritual," it becomes harder for us to see those negative traits within us that we are being called to examine. We've allowed a layer of "dust" to settle, so we must remove that dust, layer by layer, to see those things that are important for us to cleanse and transform.

Even those of us who are trying to climb a spiritual ladder and increase our ability to share will fall. It isn't a straight climb to the top. There is no direct route. The important thing to remember is that the further we fall, the higher we can rise, but it's up to each one of us to pull ourselves up by our bootstraps when we fall and not wallow in victim hood.

The 99 Percent Reality is consciousness. Science says the 99 Percent Realm is the immaterial world; it lacks physicality. It cannot be detected or measured by the physical senses. But not only does it exist, it takes up 99 percent of the Universe—despite the fact that we can not see it.

For 3400 years, our refusal, either knowingly or through ignorance, to address this 99 Percent Realm has given Satan an open field, without any opposition. He has been dedicated 24 hours a day to instilling everything of a negative nature into our consciousness by convincing us that there is no 99 Percent. He has been committed to making us do things that we sometimes suspect are wrong, but we do them anyway. The proof is in the pudding—just look around us. Illness runs rampant; chaos still exists. Nothing has changed. Why? Because Satan has been busy limiting our connection to the 99 Percent Realm. No one has ever tried to oppose him, except for the 36 righteous people whose spiritual work is the pilot light that keeps this world going.

Today, we are fortunate because, through the wisdom of Kabbalah, we have been given access to that 99 Percent Realm with our consciousness. We don't have to be limited by our five senses and the 1 Percent Illusionary Reality. Today, we have an opportunity to use the 72 Names of God and other tools like *Ana Bekho'a̱h* to do battle with Satan and to reach into and connect to the Realm of the 99 Percent—now, finally, after 3400 years!

e must have humility and know that, without the Creator, we are nothing.

hen we ask God to wash away something negative in our lives, but we are not asking for the right reasons and with the right consciousness, then the cleansing will not happen. This is because it's our thought-consciousness that needs to be cleansed, not the negative act or situation itself.

All of us are very spiritual when things are going right. But when things go wrong, we throw everything we know out the window. So how spiritual are you when the going gets tough?

All of us have the ability to climb the mountain and to face any challenge, yet we allow Satan to fill our heads with doubts like: "You can't make it. You won't get there. Give up while you can." Choosing the high road when things aren't going our way—that's what spirituality is really about.

e all want to do what we say we're going to do. We have such good intentions, but life gets in the way. Things come up; we get distracted; time goes by; we think of other things. It happens to all of us. No matter how important something is to us, sometimes we simply don't make it a priority. Maybe it's a task that requires a lot of effort, or maybe the timing isn't right. But if something is truly important, we must make the commitment and stay focused, and take the actions we need to take—even if it means going the extra mile. Taking action generates the extra energy we need to overcome whatever obstacles arise.

od translates our prayers based on our actions.

We are often unaware of when we are a slave and when we are free. Usually when we think we are a slave, we are really free, and when we think we are free, we are really a slave. For example, it is very challenging for people who are born into families of affluence. They think they are born free, but they are often slaves to materialism. Because they didn't work for what they own, they have Bread of Shame (the shame of receiving something without earning it), which often makes it even harder for them to break free of the chains that bind them.

What is the difference between an angel and a righteous person? An angel appears in order to complete one specific task. A righteous person, on the other hand, is someone who lives in this world and has turned the negativity of his existence into Light. He has made himself both whole and holy by transforming his internal nature. Therefore, a righteous person can petition the Creator on our behalf.

hrough the miracle of God—the pathway to spirituality—we can bind together. Only this bond between people lasts; everything else in the material world deteriorates. The light of a candle doesn't diminish as we light other candles. By our coming together and lighting the candle of the person next to us, the Light is amplified and the bond is made stronger—and we become a part of the miracle.

hat must one do to become spiritual? He must sweat for it, work for it, fall down, cry, and pick himself up for it. Then he must do it all over again. A person is only spiritual when he goes through the test of fire.

When Moses received the Ten Utterances (traditionally known as the Ten Commandments) on Mount Sinai, a conversation took place between him and God. Moses confessed that he had not realized how bad the situation at the bottom of the mountain had become. The Israelites had created an idol, and darkness prevailed.

God said to Moses, "In My hand, and from My mouth, the people cannot accept My message. They are not able to take the Light that would come from Me directly."

Like the people who could not accept the Laws of the Creator, we sometimes are unwilling to accept wisdom imparted to us by others. We visit with our spiritual mentor and receive an answer to a question that has been on our mind. But we don't like the answer we're given, so we disregard the entire message. Then later on, when life starts kicking us around, we realize that we received the answer we needed *a long time ago*—we just hadn't realized its worth until now.

God recognized this. He saw that the people were not ready because they were too afraid of the tremendous Light energy. But He knew exactly what they needed and how they needed to receive it.

Sometimes in our effort to be "spiritual," we inadvertently force our wisdom down someone else's throat and wind up turning them away from the very spirituality that we want to share. We can't coerce others into believing what we believe; we can only be models of the spiritual principles we are learning. There is only one way to share a spiritual message, and that is if we live our lives as better human beings. When our actions and attitude have changed, others will notice. The biggest lesson here is this: It doesn't matter how much we pray or the specifics of our spiritual practice—what is important is that what comes from us is a spiritual energy.

We are so in a hurry that sometimes we forget to experience the tender little moments that, had we paused for them, we might have saved us and others a great deal of hurt. Sometimes we are in such a rush that we forget that kindnesses along the way have more value than the goal we are trying to reach. Our life is in essence only a bundle of the things that we have done that have brought pleasure to others. And in these moments, we reach the Light of the Divine.

Each of us has unique gifts, and it is our responsibility to make use of these gifts and to share them with others. Each day, we need to do at least one action of real sharing by using the gifts we've been given by the Creator to positively impact another human being.

The smallest letter of the Hebrew alphabet, the one that comprises all the other letters, is the letter *Yud*. Although it is the smallest of all letters—it is the most powerful of all things, for it is the first letter of the Divine Tetragrammaton and contains the entire energy of the Hebrew alphabet.

There is so much bad in the best of us, and there is so much good in the worst of us, that there is no possibility of finding fault in anyone.

here are many times when our "heart is hardened," for example, when a friend we've had for many years does something to offend us. Suddenly we forget all the good times we shared and all the wonderful things our friend has done for us. We don't keep a notebook, as the Creator does, of all the good things that a person has done for us. The Creator takes into account all of our actions and doesn't single out the negative ones as we are prone to do. He judges our lives based on the net value of the love we've shared with others. Let's strive to have this same consciousness with our friends and loved ones.

hen the *Zohar* discusses the eleven fabrics that were used as the walls of the Tabernacle, it is talking about a protective covering that chaos cannot penetrate. The *Zohar* says that we all have such a protective shield; the only way we die from a heart attack, lung cancer, or any other disease is when we become vulnerable and permit Satan to enter through this protective barrier. The second we give him an opening, Satan says, "How can I get rid of this guy?" Once he has entered, all he must do is decide how he is going to drag us to our death.

But we don't have to experience disease or chaos—if we can get rid of Satan. That's what the eleven fabrics in the story are about. By fortifying ourselves, by taking care to keep our protective shield intact, we can get rid of Satan before he has a chance to enter. It is when we behave towards others with anything less then tolerance and human dignity that we puncture holes in our protective shield. This is why love thy neighbor as thyself is not just a moral way to live, but also a smart way to live.

Sometimes in order to reach a place of our correction, we have to be cleansed. One of the ways we are cleansed is by experiencing great difficulty.

Nothing in this world worth having is achieved without effort. If it were, then we would experience what the kabbalists call "Bread of Shame." With Bread of Shame, there's very little spirituality and no fulfillment because true spirituality takes work.

Each person is a world unto himself, and every group extends their vibration outward. We extend our vibration to one another, to our communities, and to the whole world. Each and every action we take is like a prayer. Our actions are what will be passed on to the rest of the world. We can extend our energy outward to share or to harm. The choice is up to us.

We are all given a gift. What we do with our gift can remove the karma we have from a previous life and help us to ascend the ladder of opportunities. Our spiritual work is to reveal all of the Light that was originally placed in our Vessel and then to become a beacon of Light for others.

The job of spreading human dignity must be something each one of us advocates. We so quickly forget that the only way we can bring about peace is by being peaceful. We have the strength; we have the numbers. But more than that, we have the consciousness to take this energy back to our communities and to talk to people about using peace instead of physical might, to focus on food, shelter, and education instead of building bombs. Your job and my job are the same: to spread the idea of human dignity and kindness to each and every person in everything we do. The *Zohar* explains we will finish the job in one of two ways: either in a big ball of fire or when each man loves his neighbor so that all will know the glory of God.

One of the most important lessons we can learn is the lesson of empathy—to be able to feel what another is feeling. The only way we can have empathy is to open up our hearts.

There is a simple story about a king who was fleeing his city during a revolution that can give us many lessons.

When the soldiers came looking for him to kill him, he ducked into a tailor's shop. "Hide me!" he begged.

"Quickly!" said the tailor, "Hide under this pile of clothing."

The soldiers entered the shop and shouted, "Is the king hiding here?" They stabbed the pile of clothing, missing the king by mere inches.

When they left, the king said to the tailor, "Thank you for saving my life. I am certain this revolution will fail, and when it does, I will grant you three wishes."

The tailor was delighted and he began, "As my first wish, I would like you to proclaim a National Tailors'

Day. My second wish is that every tailor be paid double." The tailor stopped and thought for a moment. "Before I tell you my third wish, there is one thing I would like to know. When these people were trying to kill you, how did you feel?"

The king was startled by the tailor's question and said, "You question the emotions of the king? How dare you!" When his guards came and informed him that the revolutionaries had been captured, the king had the tailor arrested. Brought to the gallows, the tailor, terrified, couldn't imagine why he was being treated this way.

Just before they were about to hang the tailor, the king said, "Release him." He then turned to the tailor and said, "Now you know what it feels like!"

The lesson is this: We might think we know what others are going through, but we really don't. Until we can genuinely feel their pain, we cannot truly become a higher spiritual being.

During the time a soul is in the womb, it is guided by angels who tell it why it has come back into this world and what kind of life it will experience. When the child emerges from the womb—at the moment the head crowns—all is forgotten until the age of 12 for a girl and 13 for a boy. At this time, the ability of the child to remember the perfection of its soul is awakened, and all of the information that the angels taught him is available to him. The child becomes an adult and a complete Vessel that can reveal the Light of God.

All physical reactions begin with a thought. For example, when someone gives you a compliment, you blush. What causes that rush of energy? That rush of energy starts with a mental seed. The blush was merely the effect; the thought or feeling you had in relation to that compliment is really where it all began.

simple *light*

I t is within our power—the power of the human race—to be able to create energy that will bring dignity and respect to all human beings. It is also in our hands to destroy it. What was the intention of the Creator when He created man? To give His beneficence to all of humanity. Therefore, everything that is negative in this world is because of the human *Desire to Receive for the Self Alone*, which means that it is within the power of every single one of us to temper that desire and to bring about the end of destruction and misery. So many people have been killed in the name of religion. How many of us in the name of spirituality can put the world back together again?

here are differing opinions out there regarding what a Spirit Guide is. Some say it's the Higher Self, while others say it's a type of consciousness. Call it what you will, but each and every one of us has heard that quiet inner voice, even though we might have disregarded it. Oftentimes, we ignore it because it is telling us something that we do not want to hear. It might be saying, "I know this man seems like a good match for you, but maybe you should wait and find out more before moving ahead with a partnership." I know we don't want to listen sometimes, but the information that is being revealed to us is well worth heeding. For our Spirit Guide is there to help lead us away from darkness and bring us closer to the Light.

e should be faster and more capable than any computer in the world, but we're not. That's because we use only a fraction of our brain's capacity. We're so bogged down with mental junk and negativity that we spend most of our time separated from the Lightforce. But no computer can run properly without a steady influx of energy.

he *Zohar* says that the lungs have the power to balance the fire of the heart. But the lungs need air and the freedom to expand. The *Zohar* adds that the lungs need to be able to share their life force in order to function. So it is no surprise that when a person feels confined by their circumstances, they experience breathing problems.

Oftentimes, people don't understand spirituality in the same way they do physicality. In the physical realm, there is an expression "No pain, no gain," which is to say "Get out there, sweat, stretch yourself. Feel the burn. Feel it. Then you will become stronger." The spiritual world works the same way. You have to feel it. You have to question. You have to work for it.

We spend a lot of time asleep not only when we are lying in our beds at night, but also during the hours we are awake. So much of the time, we are disconnected from living. We need to start injecting life into each day, acknowledging our blessings and sharing them with others.

any people will look at a picture and think, "What a beautiful picture! What a blessing it is, this beautiful picture!" But before we can appreciate a beautiful picture, we must have eyes with which to see it. How often do we acknowledge the blessing of even being able to see the beauty that is before us? All too often, we take the real blessings of the Creator for granted.

ach one of us has many opportunities during our day to remove these veils. A simple "How are you?" to someone who is trying to catch our attention during our busiest moment is all that it takes. When we extend ourselves even just a little, we open the door to the Light.

The month of *Elul*, which precedes *Rosh Hashana*, is like the labor period and the time when we have to be the most conscious of our actions, as it sets the stage for the work we will do on *Rosh Hashana*. Kabbalah explains that the holiday of *Rosh Hashana* is actually a window of time where all the souls of humanity have a chance to plug into the Source of Light that will grant us life, sustenance, and children for the coming year.

During *Elul* (the cosmic month of Virgo), the door to the Light of the Creator is slightly more ajar than at any other time of the year. This is an opportunity for us to have more direct contact with the Light. But we must also remember that the door is open to the Negative Side as well. So we must be careful to strip away our veils of negativity first in order to take full advantage of the warmth of the Light.

The world is evolving and changing, and with this change comes much chaos. The weather is going crazy, and so, too, are people, it seems. Why is this? We understand that right before the dawn is the darkest part of the night. Now, more than ever before, we have the ability to enact change. The Lightforce is the only energy that can bring an end to the chaos. Each one of us represents that Godlike force. Each of us has a piece of the Creator inside of us. When we share and treat everyone with dignity, we reveal the piece of the Creator that is part of us. I'm not saying we should be friends with everybody. But I am saying that each person—no matter who they are—is a part of the energy of the Godforce, and we must treat that individual with human dignity, no matter what.

We are born into an environment that allows us—the seed that we are—to grow and to manifest all that we are meant to. But it is up to us to do the watering. It is up to us to climb and to grow towards Heaven.

The Revelation of the Bible on Mount Sinai was more than the giving of a book, a religion, or a philosophy—it was the fulfillment of every dream a person could have ever imagined. This all-inclusive wisdom of the Universe included the keys for eternal happiness; the tools for overcoming chaos, pain, and suffering; the power of total healing, both physical and mental; the secrets for achieving personal fulfillment; and the tools for achieving immortality. Kabbalah teaches that this Revelation was for all of mankind and not just for a select few. This is because the Creator is Endless and shares His wisdom without limitation or judgment.

verybody has a way to demonstrate their personality, and it is often by the way they dress and the way they look. There are certain people, for instance, for whom clothing is very important. This is because they lack self-confidence; they feel that appearance is all they have, so appearance is what they can and will present to the world. Of course, people should be able to dress nicely and present themselves nicely. But the point is to understand for ourselves *why* we do what we do. And that "why" is related to the personality of the person.

If a person chooses to wears clothing that is different from what they usually wear, but they wear that "different" clothing for a while, this physical change will affect their personality. The reason is that there is energy in everything that exists around us. When you change how you dress or even the colors that you wear, it will have an influence on your traits and behavior. Each of us may be looking to become more attuned with the Light, but first we have to become more aware of what our issues are.

here are two types of anger: One is parent anger; the other, critical anger. Parent anger arises from a sense of nurturing. We tell someone that they shouldn't have done something because we don't want them to experience the consequences of those actions. Critical anger, on the other hand, does not come from a place of nurturing, but rather from a place of judgment.

There are also two ways that we react when others are angry with us. One is withdrawal, but when we withdraw, we disrupt the circuit of energy. Our other response to anger is spontaneous retaliation. Here, we answer immediately, which means we are sure to have a quarrel with the other person.

There is only one way to respond to anger, and that is to learn how to be proactive, taking the situation to another level. It means that when another person is angry, we don't take on their anger. We pause for a second and say, "I might be right or I might be wrong. Let's see how we can talk this thing through." In this way, we are walking away, both physically and emotionally, from the other person's reactivity.

When we think reactively with our Ego, arguments occur. But if we are proactive, there can be no argument because our Ego is not involved.

*P*eople communicate through brainwaves. Brainwaves travel in almost the same way as sound. The reason we don't pick up on these vibrations is not because we can't, but because we block ourselves by what we *think*. Rational thoughts—our intelligence—block us from our intuition.

Try this: When you are talking with someone, let go of all of the parameters that normally surround your thoughts. Allow thoughts to just come to you—right, wrong or indifferent. In this way, you can learn to achieve a level of telepathic ability, but this ability has to come from the place of non-intelligence. What does this mean? It means you become a channel for energy, which allows you to reach the energy vibration of somebody else.

I don't mean that you should block your conscious, rational thoughts. The minute you do that, you've lost the connection. If you are busy thinking, "What am I supposed to say?" then you are still in your head. You are not *supposed* to say anything—that's the point.

A prison is anything that confines us or turns us into a slave. It is also anything that keeps us separated from the Light of the Creator.

According to the *Zohar*, Egypt was a place of negative consciousness, which is why Moses did not want to pray there. From this, we learn that when we pray or when we want to connect with the Creator, we should find an environment that is positive in which to do so.

Every letter of a language has a unique vibration. When you listen to a reading from the Bible, the most important thing is to listen to the words, because when you're hearing the words of the Bible, you're hearing the music of the Universe.

any women do not recognize the responsibility they have to fill their Vessel with the Lightforce of God. They are still looking for physical avenues in which they can rebuild and rejuvenate their Vessel, but that is not what the Vessel was intended to hold. We have a choice: We can either fill our Vessel with all of the non-sense that's out there or fill it with the Lightforce energy.

But whatever type of energy we fill our Vessel with, this is the Light that we'll take home to our husband, our family, and everyone around us. That's the force we will share with those whom we love the most. That's why it says that a woman can destroy or a woman can build.

Just as the woman's egg has the power to mold the sperm, which will become a Vessel she brings into this world, the power to decide what type of energy will enter the home is in her hands—just as it is in my hands and yours.

There was a study done on cancer patients where researchers discovered that, oftentimes, people who contracted cancer had experienced depression four or five years prior to the manifestation of their cancer. What does this teach us? Depression depletes our energy, and when we become depleted, our thoughts become negative. These negative thoughts can manifest themselves as physical maladies. Because the physical body is the home of the spiritual body, when we are sick spiritually, this condition must also reveal itself physically.

We have to learn to love ourselves. It's important that we have a sense of self and self-worth, but not at the expense of another person.

We too easily forget the blessings that we have in our lives. Sometimes our closest friend or partner does something that annoys us, and in a second, we forget the love we have shared together. We need to be aware of our own forgetfulness so that we can catch ourselves in the moment and remember all the miracles that came before.

Moses had two sons and neither was deserving of leadership. They may have been born of his seed, but they were not of the same spiritual makeup; they lacked the essence of sharing. So Moses transferred the leadership to Joshua instead. Why did he choose Joshua? The kabbalists say that Joshua picked up a chair when it was broken, cleaned up what was dirty, and helped out where he was needed. Joshua earned his right to leadership, not by being born of a certain bloodline but through his ability to care for every detail and his ability to give of himself to others.

here are times when we want to integrate ourselves with others and think that the only way to do this is by wearing a mask. But when we mask ourselves from the world, we also mask ourselves from ourselves, thus separating ourselves from the Light inside, which is our true essence. There can be no fulfillment in living this way.

hat is the effect for someone who is wealthy and but doesn't share his wealth with others? He becomes a prisoner of his wealth. He hoards his money and doesn't spend a dime. But he is making a payment—a payment in the form of his happiness. He is turning over his happiness every day to his wealth.

*I*f we understood that there is a system for all the things that manifest in our lives and that everything is here to teach us and to bring us to a place where we can complete our correction, then we would never worry. We would know that God put us in this framework, in this body, and in this environment to be in the best position to finish our correction.

The circumstances in which we find ourselves are not meant as punishments; they are tools to help us elevate to another level of spiritual consciousness. If we truly understood this, then there would be no greed, anger, or envy because we would know that we are always exactly where we need to be.

*I*f you look closely at your happiest moments, you can be sure that there was someone there to enjoy them with you. That's why we are here—to share our joy and Light with one another.

If someone steals, he is sure to steal again. This is because a person who steals from others lives in a constant state of want. But life is a boomerang, and the energy we send out will return to us. If someone constantly robs energy from others, he will constantly feel robbed himself.

Kabbalists ask why the Revelation happened in the desert as opposed to a city. The reason is that the desert has no borders or boundaries. There is no personal property in a desert. Everyone is equal; everything is open; and a person can go in any direction without anyone ever stopping them. In other words, the desert represents absolute freedom. This is why so many evolved ideas could have developed only in the desert and why so many great people went into the desert for inspiration.

We shouldn't run after negativity. If there is someone in your life who is particularly negative, it is better to avoid that person. Being with a negative person or in a negative space siphons your energy and your power. It is best to steer clear of such people and places.

If we think about it, we rarely go to God when we're happy, when we're enthralled with life, when everything is going great. Instead, we go to the Creator only when we have problems. Why would we not share our happiness with the Creator when it is from Him that our happiness comes?

pirituality doesn't exist only in the temple where we pray; nor does it exist only in our prayers. Spirituality is learning to let go of a person who is nasty, jealous, and envious, and to learn to say, "That's his karma, and it's just between the Creator and him." Another person's karma is not our problem. If we take it on, we delay the removal of pain and suffering from the collectivity of humanity and we therefore delay our own destiny.

ometimes you meet your soul's other half, but it isn't at the right time or place on your journey. You might meet briefly in passing and then bump into one another again a couple of years later. New circumstances bring you together.

It's important to remember that how you present yourself to the world is how you will be remembered. As we all know, it's not possible to make two first impressions, so make your words and actions count when you meet someone. You might be the one who makes the difference in their life!

To be completely attuned to another person's "wavelength," we must completely remove our prejudices from the picture. What I see with my eyes isn't what you see with yours. You and I have two completely different perspectives on everything surrounding us. If we can temporarily give up what we think, who we are, and what we feel, we'll be able to truly hear what is being said and reach into the depths of another human being.

If, according to Kabbalah, we are all a part of the Godforce, then what right do we have to pass judgment on others? And if we are all connected, then if I judge another, am I not ultimately judging myself?

It takes only one small candle to bring light to a darkened room. We have the power to be that small light every time we choose to make a difference in one person's life. Being that candle doesn't require a great deal from us—it's the way we smile, the way we take a moment to help, the way we say, "Thank you." These seemingly insignificant actions can make a tremendous difference. This is what it means to be that one candle that shares its Light with the entire room.

ometimes we want our friends to experience the same things as we do on our spiritual path. We want them to become more involved; we want them to become spiritual. But they don't always want to hear what we have to say. "What can I do?" I am often asked. The answer goes back to what Rav Ashlag once said: "There is no such thing as coercion in spirituality." This means that even though something may be working for you, unless someone asks for your help or wants to know what you have learned, there's little benefit in trying to tell them.

This same philosophy holds true for everything in life. We are surrounded by people, who are suffering spiritually, emotionally, and physically. Oftentimes, we know of solutions that could change their life, but they aren't open to the knowledge we have to offer. The reason for this is that they are often very young souls with limited experience in this world. They are not yet on the spiritual level that is required to take in the wisdom that is available to them.

ike astrological signs, every color has both positive and negative attributes. Colors also represent a part of an individual's personality, and you can tell a lot about people by the colors they enjoy wearing. Many spiritual people like blue and green because these colors represent a willingness to expand and learn. Red is a more difficult color. It means that there is a place in the person's personality where they feel stuck. Those who connect with red are fiery; it is also difficult for them to take hold of new ideas. Black and white are opposite sides of the same coin. Black is the color of receiving—absorbing both the positive and negative of life—while white reflects all things, representing the aspect of sharing.

Each one of us has an aspect of the *Desire to Receive* inside us. But to connect to the Light of the Creator, we must be willing to give up some of our physical desires. Are we prepared to give up the natural desires we have? The amount of Light that can enter our bodies is directly proportionate to the amount of selfish desire we let go of. But we have to be willing to make room for the Light, because if we aren't willing to make room for it, we can't ask why we aren't receiving it.

When something doesn't go our way or we are fed up, we may take out our frustration on someone. This negative energy catapults to the next person whom the person we wronged comes into contact with, and the negative energy continues down the line. It might not seem like a big deal when we do it, but one reactive incident creates a domino effect.

Intuition, clairvoyance, and feeling are all right-brain functions. In fact, anything that deals with emotions and sensitivity is a right-brain function. The left brain is responsible for intellect and judgment. And where does most of the feminine functioning generally come from? It comes from the right brain. This means that women are innately more spiritual and sensitive to emotion than men are. This is why if you look in any group where people are studying spirituality; you'll usually find more women than men.

This also means that people who are truly spiritual are less judgmental because they are relying primarily on the right side of the brain for function. When a person is judgmental, they are engaging the intellectual left brain. And where you have the intellect engaged, you don't have the spirit engaged.

In the biblical Story of Exodus, there is a request made for money to build the Tabernacle—the place for the Lightforce of the Creator to dwell. However, the Israelites are unaware that their consciousness when they make a donation of money will manifest itself in the end result.

The *Zohar* says "all people with contributing heart," which refers to people who give with the right consciousness. If your consciousness is one of a tolerant individual, then the actions that you take in the physical world will reflect that tolerance. In the same way, if your donation is made with an open heart, then the physical manifestation of that donation will reflect the essence of sharing. This is what the biblical story describes—constructing the Tabernacle with the knowledge that the structure will reflect the consciousness from which it is built.

When God said, "I want a place where I can dwell," He was not referring to a physical place. It's ludicrous to think that God needs a pillow where He can lay His head down and rest a bit! He says, "Build Me a Tabernacle so that I can rest amongst you, the people." We are the Tabernacle! That is why the *Zohar* says that for those who have the ability to connect to the totality of the Lightforce, a real physical Temple can exist.

simple *light*

As the writings of Rav Ashlag tell us, "You can feed the body, but if you don't feed the soul you are empty."

The reason we wear white on days of spiritual connection is so that we may have greater affinity with the Lightforce of God. Many other spiritual teachings and cultures wear white as well. In this way, we are all the same: the amount of money in our bank accounts or where we buy our clothes becomes irrelevant—everyone is equal. Each and every day, we have the ability to bring this feeling of unity to the rest of the world.

hen we decide to become spiritual, we have to take from the past what is real and leave everything else behind. It's like taking a shower and putting on clean clothing: If a person is trying to get close to God, he has to allow himself to be cleansed before he can put on new spiritual clothing. So the next time you experience a challenge, stop for a moment and remind yourself that God is only trying to encourage you to take a shower!

The Hebrew word for one, *ehad*, has the numerical value of 13. So, too, do the Hebrew words for *love* and *care*. Therefore, to become one with another, we must have love and care for the other person. If we can't care, we don't have love. The opposite is also true: If we don't love, we can't care.

To care for someone is to want to feel closeness with that person. We are saying, "I want this person to be a part of me; therefore, I should try my best to relate to him—in his language, on his level." When we are coming from this type of consciousness, we show how much we care.

To be caring is to create unity, but in order to accomplish this Oneness, we must be prepared to give up our desired level of comfort to create a bridge between us and the other person. If we are unable to bridge the gap—if we can't move outside of ourselves and see the other person's needs—then it isn't love.

omen are the nurturers of the world. Our role is to form the foundation for the spirituality that enters our homes, our places of work, our lives. May all women find their voices so their spiritual abilities will be heard louder than ever before throughout the world.

hen asked the question: "How can I raise my child to be all they can be?" I usually answer, "It is how you are in the raising of the child that will make all of the difference." This is to say that a child learns by our actions. If there is anger and resentment, the child learns anger and resentment. If there is love and sharing, the child learns loving and sharing.

he *Zohar* says when the Tabernacle was completed, Moses checked over everything both inside and out so that there would be an accurate account. But the people saw this attention to detail as suspicious. They thought Moses was rich because he took care of the accounting and was pocketing some of the money. Who in their right minds would think that Moses would steal the money? But that was their consciousness. The reality couldn't have been further from their accusations. In fact, when Moses balanced the accounts, he was missing 1,776 shekels, and God had to come down and remind him of where he had misplaced the money. While Moses was busy taking care of others, God took care of him.

od doesn't make deals, but we try to make deals with God all the time. What does this mean? Sometimes we say, "I will pray three times a day and be a religious person if you will do this one thing for me, God." Then we question why God isn't manifesting what we want in our lives, even though we are doing all of the "right" things.

The reason we aren't getting what we want is because we are trying to make deals. In this world, the only deal is to be the very best human being that we *can* be. To achieve this level of enlightenment is the only task that God has given us to do. He wants us to wake in the morning and not only see the beauty of the world, but appreciate and marvel at how wonderful it is that we can see at all. This is the consciousness we were put on Earth to have.

e see so much craziness in the world—shootings, disease, and chaos everywhere. This is the world we live in, and it is our little actions that start the negativity that builds into this chaos. It is the reactions of all of us, millions of us—forgetting, not paying attention, not caring about the next guy—that accumulate to create this global negativity.

ife is full of ups and downs. When we are down, we question the existence of the Light, but the reason there is no Light is because we're not allowing it in. Our envy, jealousy, and anger block the Light from coming into our lives. To connect to the Light, we have to understand that the dark times are opportunities for us to collect our negative energy and transform it.

But remember that Satan doesn't want us to reach this level of consciousness, so we need to decide right now to cling to our spirituality and to fight our Satan. As long as the down is not as far as the up, we are winning the war.

here is a prayer in the morning, called *Shaharit* which in English means "darkness." Why was this prayer not called *boker*, which means "morning"? The answer is beautiful. When is the darkest part of the night? It is just before the dawn. So the reason the prayer is called *Shaharit* is because only through our darkness—that is, all of the negativity and garbage that we are all born with—can we reveal the Light.

We are all part of the darkness called *Shaharit*. That's why the world looks the way it does, with the acid rain, the air and water pollution. Through the years, we have been living in so much greed, envy, and anger that a toxic environment is the only possible result. The only way we can change this is by transforming ourselves spiritually.

We are at the pivotal point—just before the dawn. The *tzaddikim*, or righteous people, are people such as ourselves. These are the people who walk through the streets with their heads held high, ready to fight to save the world from destruction.

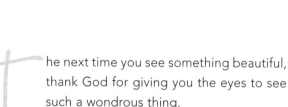

he next time you see something beautiful, thank God for giving you the eyes to see such a wondrous thing.

ost of us hear, but we don't listen. We argue, we defend, but we don't listen. Listening means waiting that extra moment and recognizing that another person may have their own way of doing things, and that if we were that person and came from where they came and with the same circumstances, we would probably think just as they do. Understanding this is the true nature of listening. Our job is to not judge another's actions; our job is to listen beyond the words.

ow many times in our lives have we said to God, "To heck with spirituality! What has it done for me?" If you listen closely, you'll hear the Creator whispering back, "Why are you complaining? Move forward and push yourself even harder!"

What has happened is that we've forgotten that the higher we climb up the spiritual ladder, the harder we have to work.

o rise above the *Desire to Receive for the Self Alone* to a higher level of consciousness is what prayer is all about.

he journey to become more spiritual doesn't happen without some kind of pain. In order to grow, we have to face and overcome certain challenges. A piece of coal remains a piece of coal unless it is put under intense pressure. Only then can it become a diamond. We all aspire to become a better version of who we are in this moment, but this can't happen unless we are willing to experience challenges. The journey to becoming a spiritual being—the diamond version of ourselves—doesn't happen without experiencing the pressure of pain.

iriam, the sister of Moses, contracted leprosy because she inadvertently said something against Tsipora, the wife of Moses. It's important to remember that although her words were not intentional, they still had a negative effect. Speaking about another "inadvertently" is no excuse under the Universal Law of Cause and Effect.

hen someone pushes your buttons, ask yourself this: "Is this person someone I truly want to be with?" And if this person is, then you must make a conscious choice to bypass the rest of the garbage.

e all have a predetermined amount of time to be here on Earth, as well as a pre-determined number of words and actions to use in our lifetime. Positive actions such as studying spirituality and helping others, speaking positive words, and giving encouragement, do not get charged against our account; however, when we speak negatively, those words are counted. Therefore, by making every action we take and every word we speak positive ones, we have the ability to create immortality.

e all have a predetermined amount of time to be here on Earth, as well as a pre-determined number of words and actions to use in our lifetime. Positive actions such as studying spirituality and helping others, speaking positive words, and giving encouragement, do not get charged against our account; however, when we speak negatively, those words are counted. Therefore, by making every action we take and every word we speak positive ones, we have the ability to create immortality.

he *Zohar* refers to the Gates of Mercy that open and close, but there is one Gate that can always be opened—the Gate of Tears. When we cry out to God and ask for His help to become more spiritual, the Gate of Tears swings open wide. A miniscule tear is the drop of Light needed to take us to the next level. It allows us to climb to where God is, and it is in this place, we understand that we are surrounded by opportunities to grow better. When we cry to God with the desire to become more than we are today, the Gate of Tears is open. But if we cry out to God with selfishness, desiring more for our selves alone—for the Mercedes that our neighbor drives, for more money—the Gate of Tears is closed to us.

For me, the decline of religion dates back to the time when the Temple stood and High Priests would try to buy their way into the Holy of Holies without giving of themselves in service. This happens today. Many people give a nice contribution of money or goods, but what do they give of themselves? Each one of the kabbalistic tools we use is designed to take us to a higher dimension; simple monetary contributions made without the act of giving of oneself cannot achieve this.

What is it that keeps us apart from God and what brings us closer to God? The answer lies in the *mikveh*, a spiritual cleansing bath. Every negative action we take creates a veil; each veil separates us further and further from the Lightforce. But the *mikveh* can lift these veils and bring us closer to God. When we immerse ourselves in the cleansing water of the *mikveh*, we return to the amniotic fluid of our divine womb and become connected to the pure version of ourselves that existed before we made choices that resulted in the negative energy and veils that surround us now. This is the purpose of the *mikveh*.

Everyone has the ability to be a healer. The hands contain the most energy in the body, which is why people like to be held and touched. Babies love to be massaged because it calms them down. The only time our hands lack healing energy is when we have been in a house where there has been sickness and we've failed to wash our hands afterwards. We also lack healing powers when we have been with negative people. Negative energy can greatly undermine our healing powers. It's also important to remember that we should wash our hands properly before performing healing work on another.

here is a story of a man who had a teacher for 15 years. He said to his teacher, "Lately, I feel as though I have been unable to find answers to my questions. The teacher responded, "That's because you stopped asking the questions and found your own answers instead." Like the student, sometimes we think that we already know the answers. But when we have this mindset, we are unable to hear real wisdom when it is given to us.

ll of us here on Earth are full of so much cosmic debt. For that reason, there is so much negativity on Earth, so many diseases, so many catastrophes. It is for us—you, me, and everyone else—to direct and change that energy. Because we are here, we are responsible. Now is our chance. Have you noticed that there are more spiritual shows on television than ever before? We, as a people, are hungry for spiritual knowledge and tools, and we are seeing now, more than ever before, that there is a reason for our existence.

The things that fill us with Light can only come from a spiritual root. Money, possessions, and honor cannot fill us with Light. True fulfillment can only come when our soul is satisfied that we are doing the real work—the spiritual work of transforming ourselves. As long as we are in our physical body, our work is not yet complete.

There have been many times when I have asked myself why I continue to do this work when there are so many people who hate me for it. I continue because I know that this is my life's work and there is more for me to do.

he *Zohar* says that anything we ask of the Lightforce we must be prepared to work for. If we want a miracle to save us, we have to make the opening through which the miracle can enter.

If we say, "I've done all this; now where is the miracle?" or "I'm not worried because I'll be saved," then we are sure to be disappointed. No person—not even Moses—can depend on their deeds or rest on their laurels. We have to be willing to create our own miracles.

So many people remain in situations that make them feel miserable. They stick it out because they don't know how to change their circumstances. We stay in a relationship that's no good, but we think it is easier than being alone. We stay in an unfulfilling job for the same reason. Most of us are a slave to something. But when we live in bondage to a situation or a person, we leave no space for the Light of the Creator to do His work.

The *Zohar* says that there are two kinds of people: God's servants and God's children. The *Zohar* explains that the difference between a servant of God and a child of God is that the servant performs his tasks dutifully. He prays, performs good deeds, and is charitable. He does these things because they are what is expected of him. He does these things so that he'll be considered one of the good people.

What, then, is a child of God? A child of God does everything from a spiritual consciousness. He does it because it is what he expects of himself and not because another expects it of him. Everything he does is in order to connect to the Lightforce of God.

he Bible tells us that a person who gives of himself must do so with joy. If we aren't performing our actions and deeds with joy, then at some level, we are still thinking of ourselves.

rom a spiritual perspective, the words "rich" and "poor" are understood differently. To be poor means to lack Light, and to be rich means to be endowed with much wisdom.

ne day, all the world will understand the bottom line, and it is this: When an Arab child is hurt, an Israeli mother must cry for that child, and when an Israeli child is hurt, the Arab mother must also cry. So must it be. When we bleed, our blood runs the same color, no matter what the color of our skin or the religion of our upbringing.

ccording to the great kabbalists, fasting on Yom Kippur is a cosmic opportunity for all of humanity to disconnect from the world of the physical and move to the higher level of consciousness known as the *Sefira* of *Bina*, where there is no time, space, or motion. If we accept that fasting raises our spiritual consciousness by letting us disconnect from the desires of the body, we also recognize that we become the Cause and not the Effect. When we take this cosmic opportunity to raise our consciousness, we create a consistency within the Vessel and our soul becomes connected to the Lightforce of God. We are then able to rise above our current spiritual consciousness and connect with *Bina*. From that place, we are able to recognize our actions as negative, and thus we are protected from becoming consumed by our negativity. Fasting on Yom Kippur allows us to rise above the physical plane, to see our worldly actions for what they are and to transform them into spiritual acts. Spiritual actions are the only way to move closer to the Light. When we have this consciousness and the desire to evolve spiritually by choosing the right environment to help us grow, we are "without blemish."

Sometimes we fool ourselves into choices that make other people our scapegoats. Sometimes it's a loved one, sometimes a child, sometimes a friend or a business associate.

How do we know when we are using someone else as a scapegoat for our own negativity? When do we realize that we are the ones who need to change and not the other person? The people in our lives can show us a great deal about our own consciousness if we are only smart enough to stop for a moment and ask, "Are the people around me the problem, or is it the mind space that I'm in that's causing this negativity?" The time to ask this question is when someone says something negative to us or takes an action that hurts us deeply.

There is a story about King David going into battle. A man stood at the side of the road and as King David passed, this man started to curse him. King David said, "If he is cursing me, indeed I deserve to be cursed."

Unlike King David, usually when someone hurts us, we think first with our Ego. "Why is this person hurting me?" We ask. We cut ourselves off from the individual because he or she has invaded our space and injured our Ego. But the people who irritate us most are just mirroring our own negative traits. What we see in them exists in us as well; it's just concealed.

But what if we could learn to ask ourselves instead, "Why is this person in my movie? If he or she is doing something that is an affront to me, what lesson am I to learn here?" More often than not, life's most important lessons appear within the framework of the small details and conversations of our lives. Imagine how much more we can receive and how much more we can learn from these little insignificant actions we take for granted?"

*I*f you have a desire, a dream, and enough perseverance, the Light will help you achieve your dream. But if the consciousness behind this dream is one of selfishness, you might still achieve your goal, but this will come with a cost and you won't experience lasting fulfillment. True fulfillment is having someone say, "Thank you. You have changed my life." That's why we do it. If you dream of changing only your own life, then there will be little Light to show you the way.

*W*e are all brothers and sisters, which means that we have a mission to complete together. We are all a part of one another's *Tikkun* (spiritual correction), and we must do what we came here to do.

ne of the greatest things we are asked to do is to love God. But how do we love a Force that we cannot see or hear and that is not a part of our daily existence? Where is this God? How are we supposed to love and connect and share with Him?

Loving God means having affinity with Him; it means uniting with Him. And the only way to achieve this is to become like God—to take on the characteristics of God. To show God our love, we must take on His attribute of Loving Your Neighbor as Yourself.

This is the highest quality of love. If all of us had the ability to love our neighbor as we do ourselves, we would have already achieved purity of being. Our nature is to *take* for ourselves, not to *share* of ourselves.

So, if our nature is to take, then why does God want us to give? Why are we being asked to love our neighbor—someone who is not even close to us, someone whom we know little about? The answer is simple: When we transform our selfish nature by learning to love one another like God, we transform darkness into Light.

ruth is very simple. If a teacher can take a concept and explain it to you in a way you can understand, he probably knows what he is talking about. If it is too codified and complex, chances are he doesn't know what he is talking about.

e can eliminate our fears by going back to the time when the fear first manifested itself. We have to find the seed of fear and transform it. During our meditation time, we can ask the Creator to reveal where we were and what happened to us that made us so anxious. But when we do this kind of spiritual work, it is important that we are ready to let it go and to be in a place of wholeness and security—a place where we're connected to the Oneness of the Creator. This is the feeling that we should carry with us when we go back to that time and place. If we take this level of consciousness into our meditation, we can begin to turn our fear into Light.

corpio is one of the most powerful signs of the zodiac. Scorpios seek control and are very intelligent. They're powerful and very passionate, going to any length to get the results that they seek. This can work to their advantage or disadvantage.

Scorpios like to be in control, so during the month of Scorpio, we have to work hard to temper our desire to control, whether in a business or a personal relationship. It's also important to note that Scorpios are very sensual, but often have difficulty with the dynamics between men and women. So it's important to focus on our relationships this month. We have to be more careful at this time with our friends and our partners and work to enjoy them for who they are and not for what they can give us.

reen and blue, as you know, are healing colors, so I ask you to take the color green, place it like a swirling ball outside the center of your chest, then bring it in towards you. Now breathe in this beautiful green light. As it cleanses your internal organs, may you feel its strength and its energy giving you peace and healing in the internal parts of your body.

Violet is the color of spiritual connection and protection. For this moment again, feel your entire being vibrating in the soft glow of violet light. Feel the vibration move through your being from the top of your head down through your spine into your internal organs and then down to your feet. Now replace this violet light with a beautiful white Light. Create a cocoon with this Light, which surrounds your entire body. This is the Light of protection. Anytime you go into a crowd of people whom you don't know or to a place that is unfamiliar to you, this circle of protection will be there for you to guard against any negative forces which might exist. This beautiful white Light will remain with you always.

*n*ow would be a good time to sit quiet for a moment and to thank the Creator for allowing you the privilege of this moment of contentment.

*A*t times, when we are working spiritually, we seem to hit a plateau and things don't seem to be going the way they are supposed to go. We feel stuck. By remembering to put the Light of the Creator first in our thoughts and actions, we can overcome our plateaus and start altering our lives, editing our movies.

uring the time of the Holy Temple, there were those who lived outside the walls of the city of Jerusalem and those who lived inside the walls. Each day, a bullock would be passed from outside to inside where it would be used for the sacrifice at the Holy Temple.

One day, the people who lived outside the walls said, "We who are outside the walls do not understand why only those inside Jerusalem should receive the energy from these sacrifices." So instead of sending a bullock, they sent in a pig so that those inside would have less to sacrifice and would be deprived of God's energy. The motivation behind this action came from the thought that "If I don't have, then the next guy shouldn't have either." Sometimes our actions are based on such a belief. This is because we don't really understand that there is an infinite amount of the Creator's energy—enough for everyone.

hen you find yourself in a challenging relationship, how do you know if you should walk away or if you need to stay to find out why this relationship is in your life? I think one thing that you should do is make a list of all of the positive and negative attributes of the other person. Write down all the reasons why you chose him or her to be in your life. Then ask yourself: "When I take into account all of it—the good and the bad—would I feel a void if this person were no longer in my life? Is the challenging aspect of the relationship one that I can change and that I can help to change? Can I help him or her to grow? Can I use the spiritual teachings that have been shared with me to bring this person and this relationship to a better place?" If the answer to all these questions is yes, there is value in the relationship, and you should fight for it.

A person who sits by himself on a mountaintop, praying for four hours a day and meditating, may be a spiritual being. But true spirituality requires that we learn to connect with each another. If we can't connect with one another and share of ourselves, then we are not spiritual.

Either there will be rain and crops will flourish or there will be drought and the crops will fail. It is pretty cut and dry. It's the same with blessings and curses. When we go with the Light within us and consider other people, we are blessed. When we consider only ourselves, we are cursed.

It is said that Moses was chosen to lead the Children of Israel out of Egypt because when he was shepherding a flock, he picked up a new-born lamb and carried it. God said that if Moses could care this much for a single little lamb, how much more could he care for people.

The greatest trait of any leader is that he or she leads from the heart and not from the head. A person might be able to use great words to describe a beautiful nighttime sky, or be able to explain how the world works in terms of physics, or be able to discuss the great art of the world. But unless someone who is a leader can make decisions from the heart, neither he nor his people will be able to experience a strong connection with the Lightforce of God. The most important aspect of living is not to fill our brains with facts, but rather to fill our hearts with love—and a great leader recognizes this.

e are experiencing a time of rapid change as the ideas of space and time are dissolving. All of the change we are witnessing is leading us to one thing—the moment when we will experience the total evolution of the spirit. This is why people are more spiritually evolved and involved than ever before—spirituality has cleared away so many levels of negativity that we are now capable of seeing more than we ever did in the past.

he spiritual energy of the household, as well as the spiritual level of every soul that came forth into this world, is derived from the female aspect—from the manifestation of *Malkhut* It is through the energy of the female and the world of the physical that the rest of creation will be fed.

any people come to me asking, "Is it in my power to cure disease?" And my answer is "Yes, absolutely." But we have to become Godlike, and this is very hard. It is hard because we tend to love only the ones close to us, but this is not being Godlike. It is only natural to love what is ours; to go beyond that and to love somebody else's child can be very difficult to do. But to be Godlike and cure disease, we must learn to love *all* of God's children.

rayer is just a tool; our consciousness when we pray is the activating ingredient. If we do not know how to connect to the Lightforce during our prayers, then our prayers will not be heard.

ake a little time today and try to change one thing in your personality that you dislike. In changing that one thing in yourself, you affect change in the people around you. We don't start with the idea of changing the world, but when we make small changes in ourselves, we reveal the spark of God within us. This is what creates change in the world.

eople forget their true mission when they come to the physical world. We become distracted by material things. To overcome this, life knocks us around until we realize that the only true fulfillment comes from the non-physical things in life, such as love and contentment.

If we don't come to this realization, we will have to return to Earth over and over until we do.

he bonds that sustain communities have the power to withstand evil. Let us unite in this way.

hen we speak about stress and anxiety, we should know that the basic cause for all illness—and I mean *all* illness—does not come from the body but from the motivations of the mind. How many of you believe that a doctor heals? The doctor doesn't heal—he or she is just a tool, a channel for something higher. The body heals itself.

Let's say, for example, that you fracture a bone and go to an orthopedist. What does the orthopedist do? He takes the bone, sets it into the framework where it was before, then leaves the body to mend itself. In other words, it's not the orthopedist who mends the bone, but rather the body itself.

By the same token, we also need to understand that our brain is what causes and motivates all of the illnesses of our body.

agittarians are people who like to walk on the edge. They enjoy the challenge and the fight. They're the tightrope walkers of the world and the people who will take a chance on things that other people won't. They're the people who love life. The things that motivate Sagittarians, both in their personal lives or in business communications are often too eccentric or esoteric for most people to understand. Sagittarius is one of the nicest signs of the zodiac, but it is not without its challenges. It is very difficult to corral a Sagittarian because they have such difficulty with establishing boundaries.

Sagittarius is ruled by Jupiter, which is the planet of expansion. So if we are responsible with our dealings with people in the cosmic month of Sagittarius, we can expand that energy even further. But we must make sure that whatever we are pursuing has a solid foundation. In this way, we can assure that the proposal, business, marriage, or any other type of relationship will be successful.

od said, "Create for Me a house in which I will dwell." We ask, "Why do we need a house, a place of worship, a temple?" The answer is that only when people come together in one place for the purpose of spirituality can the energy of the Creator flow freely. Yet we can also assemble in a place of worship and still go home empty. The difference between walking away empty and walking away full is in the consciousness we bring to our worship.

emember that the problems we face today are the ladders by which we climb towards the Lightforce of God. Through our actions in the face of challenge, we can become pure. What does it mean to be pure? It means to have evolved from that which was once impure. We move closer to purity every time we slip on the ladder but manage to right ourselves and continue upward into the arms of God and His greatness.

Some of the most precious moments we have are the ones when we remember to just *be*. In those moments, if we are quiet, we hear the voice that says, "It's okay. Just be who you are and do not worry, for every time a door closes for you, another will open through which you shall go, as we approach this time of great Light."

*L*et me tell you a story about the great kabbalist, the Baal Shem Tov. Each time he would finish praying, he would greet one of the congregation with "*Shalom aleikhem*" (said when you haven't seen someone in three days). One day, one of the men in the congregation responded, "Tell me, I have never left the city, nor has my father ever left the city. Why is it when we finish praying you always say, '*Shalom aleikhem*'?"

The Baal Shem Tov replied, "Where were you while you were praying? Were you thinking about the vacation you wanted to take or the day ahead? Whatever you were thinking about, you weren't here in spirit, so I welcomed you back."

When we pray or read a holy book, our consciousness can generate energy for ourselves and for the whole world. Therefore, it is important before we pray to ask ourselves, "Am I praying for myself? Or am I praying so that the world can have more Light?"

What are our prayers like? Are they without blemish? How much of ourselves have we really given that we can stand before the Creator and beg to have a connection to the Light?

n understanding who you are, it is important to know first of all that you are Godlike. Unless you have that understanding, it is impossible for you to give Light to others or even to bring Light into everything you do. One way to connect to and share the Light is to say a sincere "Good morning" to someone, even if you don't feel great and things aren't going the way you think they should. This is one small way that you can share with those around you the Light of God that resides within you.

e need to be beacons of Light even when there is no one around to give us Brownie points for it. That is the consciousness we must bring into each day. We don't share Light, hoping for something in return—we give it unconditionally.

ore people have died because of religion. Someone, who is religious, might say that they were talking to God and that God told them to do what they did. So how do we know whether the message we hear is coming from the Light or coming from the Negative Side? We need to always ask ourselves, "How is what I'm about to do going to affect others? Is it good for the entire community? Do we want to cause friction or division among people so that we can feel stronger? If we are trying to motivate a person to act in a certain direction, is it simply because we want him to see things the way we do so we can feel right? Or is our action a sharing action that also respects the space and process or others?" We always need to check the intention behind our actions and make sure that what we're doing is coming from the Lightforce.

hat is a rich person? The word *ashir*, "rich" in Hebrew is an acronym for the words "eyes, teeth, hands, feet." That's a rich person! Someone who has eyes to see, teeth to eat and speak, hands to create, and feet to walk. This, of course, does not refer only to the physical, but to our ability to be able to connect with, to share, to create, and to do.

here were two opposing factions living in one community in the time before the Romans entered Jerusalem: One side wanted to wage war against the Romans, and the other side did not. What did the side that wanted to wage war do? They burned the food supply that should have fed the people for three years. They did this so that those who didn't want to fight would be forced to join in the war efforts. Can you imagine? They deprived their own people in order to achieve their own end. Where do we deprive others of Light in order to get our way?

*Y*om Kippur is the day that the Upper Worlds are open for all humanity to allow our prayers to be answered and our negativity to blow into the sea as if it never existed.

Spiritually, we stand before the gates of the Holy of Holies, begging for our lives, or at least for the opportunity to renew and redo that which we didn't do in the year past. As we stand here, we must not only ask for forgiveness, but be willing to give forgiveness, as well. If we are not forgiving in our nature, if we sit in judgment, if we don't value and appreciate others, we cannot stand before the Creator and ask of Him what we do not ask of ourselves. So we should think before we say our prayers and try to find in ourselves the capacity to be like the Creator—to stop judging and forgive.

We are asking the Creator to dissolve all of the negative things we have done, but He can only do this when we are willing to do the same for those around us. We must see that the Divine is in each of us, and if we can do that, it will come back to us—not only on *this* day but on *every* day. I hope the unity we will form will bring us to a place that free of chaos, pain, and suffering, and full of Light everlasting.

Spiritual beings are people who can generate Light throughout the whole world. People may speak in spiritual terms, but if their words generate divisiveness, there is usually an alternative motive. That which is truly spiritual creates the energy of oneness and unity.

After 17 years, Jacob was re-united with his son, Joseph, who was presumed dead. The years he now lived with Joseph in Egypt were the happiest for him, but Jacob had to earn those happy years. He had to transform and grow spiritually. This is our job as well. We, too, can have what Jacob had, but this joy is dependent on what we have done with our lives and whom we have touched. Our happiness is not determined by the nails we have hammered, but by the deep spiritual work we have done.

simple *light*

Sometimes people work very hard to support their families, but they spend almost no time with their children. I am not saying that we should not work to support our families, but it is just as important to spend time with them.

We need to assess ourselves every day and see where we have failed. It is important to do this on a daily basis to correct the negativity within us that needs to be transformed.

wo souls that are on an equal spiritual level, working together as a couple and as part of something bigger than themselves—this is the true essence of a soul mate relationship. To have this type of relationship with another, you both must agree on the important things: the values you hold dear must be the same, and you must both take time to support and nurture these values. A soul mate relationship feeds the soul, not just the body.

So many people long for this level of compatibility. But it's important to remember that not everyone came here to marry and find their soul mate. Many people on this Earth have important work to carry out that may have nothing to do with finding their soul's other half. Take, for example, a person like Mother Teresa who never married but cared for orphaned children and created unity in the world. Her job on Earth was to do exactly what she did.

ow do you find a soul mate? Start by asking, "Where am I looking and what am I looking for?" Chances are that a person who is over 35 or 40 and is still looking for a soul mate has probably set the bar far too high. Such a person is looking for perfection, but who of us is perfect? If we are looking for a man who is affluent, intelligent, charming, and handsome, maybe it's time to rethink our priorities and decide what is really important in a mate. Then perhaps we can find someone with whom to share our lives.

If you have something you really want to achieve and you want the help of the Light, how do you know when to pull back and let the Light in? How do you find that balance? You start by making sure that your consciousness is in the right place and that you are coming from a place of sharing. If so, then you will be successful at letting in the Light.

There are others with talent, but 90% of them won't achieve the goals they have set for themselves. Is this a problem with the Light? Or did they fall short of their dreams because they didn't let the Light in? Maybe what they envisioned isn't what they are supposed to be doing. Maybe they need to change their direction.

If your dream involves sharing your Light and gifts with the world, success is sure to follow.

Some people think that giving charity is all they have to do in order to share. It's easier to write a check and give from your bank account than it is to give of your time, your love, or your talent. But giving of yourself is the only true act of sharing Light.

If we want to be this or that by age 50, what happens every day until we reach the anticipated moment? Is every day of our life until we reach 50 a waste? When we open our eyes and breathe in the morning, we should realize that this day is just as important as any other. Our job today is no different than it was yesterday or will be tomorrow—or even 25 years from now. Our task is still to bring more Light to the world. This day—today—does matter.

The Biblical story of Korah is a wonderful story for all of us. Korah came from the Tribe of Levi, one of the 12 tribes of Israel. Korah was a very wealthy, handsome, and wise person. He had everything a person could want. Despite having it all, he formed a rebellion to turn people against Moses, one of his own tribe. Korah had great influence in his tribe and convinced 250 people to go against Moses. But his manipulation of these 250 people brought all of them, including Korah, to their deaths.

Now remember that Korah was a very wise man. Did he think there would be no consequences from his actions? Because a vision had shown him that the Prophet Samuel was to come from his line, he believed that he was destined to live. So as smart as he was, he didn't see the inevitable consequence of his actions, and he perished. His two sons, on the other hand, did not side with him. And it was from those sons that the lineage continued.

What does this teach us?

Greed offers no fulfillment. A person, who is greedy, like Korah, is always looking for more. Korah desired something that didn't belong to him: the power and leadership that was given to Moses. So instead of working with Moses, he manipulated people to turn their love for Moses into hatred.

When someone close to you hurts you deeply, how can you use that pain to benefit both yourself and the other person? The first thing you must do is distance yourself from the situation and observe your emotions. Only when you no longer feel the pain should you speak to the other person.

It says in the Bible that when Rivka sent her son Jacob away, she told him that he could return only when he no longer believed that his brother, Esau, hated him. Like Jacob, we must wait. We must step away from the situation, digest it, think about it, and ask ourselves why we attracted this kind of negative incident into our lives in the first place.

Then, especially if you are the one who is trying to become more spiritual, you should initiate an open dialog with the person who hurt you—not with another friend or someone on the outside, but directly with the person and only when you no longer feel anger. If you still feel anger, your Ego remains in charge and you will be unable to hear your loved one's response. But if you approach the other person without an agenda, you will reveal Light instead of promoting chaos, and you will grow spiritually in the process.

abbalistically, when we speak about sickness on any level, we call it dis-ease. It's disjointedness, a disharmony with the Light. What is the Light? The Light is completeness; it is totality. So what happens when we become diseased? We separate ourselves from the Light of the Creator.

ou cannot force people to open their minds and to see what is there to see. To be truly spiritual is to realize that not everybody will have the same reference point as you do. Spirituality, especially the path of Kabbalah, is not for everyone. The Light is very strong, and if a person cannot manage this kind of energy, then it is not the right path for them *at this time.*

D o you know the story about the angels who argued with God and asked Him, "Why are You giving the Bible to humans? Why give it to people who cause corruption, death, pain, and murder? Why not leave it with us? We will cherish it."

God said, "Why do you need such a tool? You are already pure. I must give this instrument to those who will use it to overcome those things you just mentioned, thereby bringing the powerful energy of My Light into manifestation. You, the angels, are to serve as My instrument, while the Bible is to serve as the people's instrument."

L etting go of Ego means listening to another completely—even when we don't agree with what they have to say. It means allowing someone to have a differing opinion—and not turning it into a war of words. It means being in a place where we recognize that we don't have to take offense—just because someone doesn't share our viewpoint.

The Bible says that when the Israelites left Egypt, Moses didn't take them out in a direct way. Instead, he led them in such a way that they wouldn't be able to find their way back to Egypt. Because of the route they took, they experienced many hardships. The lesson here is a simple one: In order to move to a higher level of spirituality, we must leave the path that we know best and venture into the unknown.

In the same way that the Israelites wanted to return to Egypt, sometimes we would prefer to go back to our own "Egypt" where we feel safe and comfortable— even if it means going back to chaos. At least there we know what to expect. On a new route, we have no idea what the results might be. Sometimes the Creator has to lead us away, down a path we know not. He doesn't give us a choice, but is for our own spiritual good, for it prevents us from returning to chaos.

*M*any people are workaholics, busy day and night, with no real time. Sometimes these people become seriously ill and find themselves with the time to reexamine the course of their life. The illness, therefore, was necessary to change the workaholic's perspective on life. He can choose to take his new perspective and plan a new course to take—one that can bring him closer to the Light of the Creator.

*M*ost of us try to be somebody we are not in order to please others. When we allow others to affect the way we present ourselves, we become blocked spiritually. But when we become aware of that blockage, we have a great opportunity to learn and grow from it.

I t is easy to lose sight of the great work that God intends for us to accomplish in this lifetime.

There is a story about a great scholar who lived some 150 years ago. He was a financial genius and spent most of his time devising systems that made him large sums of money. One night, he had a dream in which he saw two angels asking each other, "Should we show him all that he was meant to achieve in this lifetime?" They opened a curtain and there, sitting at the bottom of God's throne, was a great white angel. The angel turned to the scholar and asked, "Where are all the great spiritual books you were meant to write? Where are all the people you were supposed to reach? What have you been doing with your time?"

In his dream, the scholar saw himself replying, "I have so many things in the works." Before he could continue, the angel of God said, "I do not want to hear your excuses. Do you think I gave you a mind so you could earn a handful of gold? Do you think that is why I put you here?"

When he awoke, the scholar was deeply moved by the dream and decided to act on its message. He committed himself to fulfilling what the angels had shown him. He went on to write many great spiritual works and to establish a school with many students. The angels appeared in another dream and said, "Blessed are you in this world and the next."

How are we using the gifts the angel of God has given us?

Stress means that I don't really believe in the Lightforce of God. It means that I lack certainty. If I were looking at the Light instead of the situation in front of me, I would understand that even if I lost my job today, there would be another job that paid double waiting around the corner. So should I be stressed at this moment? No. But as long as I lack certainty, I will feel stress.

In the Book of Exodus, God told Moses that he had the ability to persuade, but Moses questioned this. Moses was a Pisces, and sometimes a Pisces prefers to hide rather than to take on responsibility. But this wasn't the case with Moses. Moses wasn't shirking responsibility. He was really asking, "Am I the channel? Am I the person you want me to be, God?" Like Moses, we are often unsure of our ability to spread Light, but despite this, it is our responsibility to be the beacon that God intends us to be.

One of the greatest ways to reveal Light is through unity within a couple. What are some of the ways for partners to create this unity? This depends on the couple in question. Sometimes it is difficult to change old habits. Many times, if one partner is studying and growing spiritually and the other person isn't, the one growing spiritually should become a model of the principles he or she is learning, rather than a teacher or lecturer. There is no such thing as coercion in spirituality. We have to learn how to talk to the other person in a way that encourages them to hear us better.

For example, if you are married to a Leo, as I am, you never tell them that something they have said or done was wrong. This is an immediate turn-off because you are affecting their Ego, and Leos have a great deal of pride in who they are. But if you take the same individual and compliment him or her, then you have a shot at encouraging them to change.

In the same manner, if you criticize a Cancer, you lose the person. But if you say, "Do you know how much you hurt me?" then you have a chance because a Cancer is sensitive to pain and hurt. Learn the psychology of how to speak to your partner for his or her own good, and your relationship will grow in the process.

A person's energy will pervade everything that is theirs. Even a book can be charged with the energy of its owner.

What is the punishment for a jealous person? Living a life with jealousy. When we are jealous, nothing is ever enough—all we feel is lack. Therefore, jealousy is both the cause and the effect of our suffering; the seed of jealousy itself is the consequence. Each day that we live with jealousy, we are in crisis. We feel entitled and cannot break free from these thoughts. Jealousy is its own punishment.

It is the female who lights the candles on Friday night. Why? It is said that the female, represented by Eve, took the Light out of the world, and therefore it is the job of the female to usher the Light back into the world.

Sometimes we mess up and wind up back here again, working on the same correction in this life as we did in our last life. But the Creator will always wait patiently and with loving kindness for our transformation.

*W*hen there are many children in the family, parents sometimes favor one child. This is what happened with Joseph. Jacob had an affinity with Joseph because they both represented Central Column energy. But by favoring Joseph, Jacob caused envy between his sons, prompting them to sell their brother Joseph into slavery. It is the job of parents to promote unity, not divisiveness, within the family.

*T*he *Zohar* says that a wife can build or destroy. Korah's wife had this power. She said to him, "Look what Moses has done to you! He shaved your hair off, and now no one knows who you are. He doesn't want you to be on the same level as he is and have the same status! But are you not entitled to it? Is this not your right?" With her words, she destroyed. It was after she spoke that Korah tried to bring down the leadership of Moses and Aaron. It is the power of the woman to either build her man up or tear him down.

When something bad happens in some place where you were supposed to have been but weren't, that's actually the Light tapping you and saying, "Hey, you just got another chance. What are you going to do with it?"

A good friend of mine survived cancer. Then he was shot in the line of duty in the army; he should have died but didn't. He had a heart attack and survived open-heart surgery. You name it—it happened to him, but he survived. Today, most of his time is spent in giving back, doing good works. Why? Because he recognized, after being tapped on the shoulder so many times, that he would have to be deaf not to hear what God was telling him. So take notice. When you are put in a place of danger and then saved from it or walk away unscathed, ask yourself: "What is the Creator trying to tell me?"

here is a story of two wise men. One of the sages was helping a man with much negativity, someone on a much lower spiritual level. The other wise man asked, "Why are you helping someone so clearly negative and not worthy of your help? After all, it is written: 'Love your neighbor as yourself,' and the word 'yourself' (*kamokha*) means someone of similar status, so there is no reason to help a lowly person."

The other sage answered, "*Kamokha* means that we need to have unconditional love for everyone."

Even those on a spiritual path can forget that in order to remove *sinat hinam*, or "hatred for no reason," we need to love everyone unconditionally.

Those of us who are more aware or perhaps more in tune with all that surrounds us should realize that this awareness is not simply a blessing in and of itself. It is an opportunity to bring other people to the same awareness. Let's not take our awareness for granted.

When we take a spiritual or elevating action, whether it's in our home, our community, our environment, or with our loved ones, we are building a spiritual home, which can develop and nurture spiritual qualities in ourselves and others.

But when we take an action that is rooted in the *Desire to Receive for the Self Alone*, we usher in another kind of energy that does not help build our spiritual home.

ust as the soul acquires a body at birth, we come to this world and make acquisitions. We acquire a spouse, children, grandchildren, and we acquire the love for children and the love for people. But these are only the tools we need to do our soul's mission in the physical world; they are not the reason we are here.

braham, one of the highest souls of humanity, came from a father who was an idol-maker. Moses was born from the sexual union of two relatives. This shows that oftentimes, there is a beautiful Light within something that seems negative; we must remove the dirt so that the Light shines through from a distant place. This concealment happens so the negativity of the Left Column, the *Desire to Receive for the Self Alone*, doesn't consume this great Light before it has a chance to grow and become its true essence. We never know from what Vessel true spirituality will come.

Today we are not at that same level spiritually as the patriarchs of the Bible. But the same principle remains true: no one really knows where great Light is going to come from.

hen we feel we are being judged by another, this is simply a mirror reflecting the judgment that we have within us and use to judge others. In the same way, that which we learn to forgive in others is what we will in turn be forgiven for. The Creator wants nothing of us except to see us acting as He would act. He would like to see us spending our moments caring for one another, loving one another. There's so little of that on our planet, so it's our job as conscious beings to strive every day to get closer to that level of awareness.

nergy is circular. When we succumb to giving the evil eye, we incite the evil eye in the other person, as well as in ourselves. When we give out anger, we get back anger. We receive the same energy that we share with the world.

The only question that will be asked of us at the end of the road is not whether we battled and won, but how we battled. The only thing that will matter will be how much love we have given to others, for we won't be judged by what we have, but by how much we have shared.

hen Abraham entertained a stranger, he did so under a palm tree. He would watch the leaves on the tree closely. If the leaves drooped, he knew the person was negative; if they went up, he knew the person was positive. We all need to pray everyday that God will open our eyes to truly see what is positive and what is negative, and our ears to hear and understand the message that is intended for us.

ou are totally capable of rising above the negative situations in your life. The more difficult your challenges, the higher you can elevate spiritually and the more the Creator must add to your spiritual weights, knowing full well that you will be able to lift them.

O ftentimes, we don't like the way our children behave. It's important to understand that we created that tree, but perhaps we didn't water it properly at the beginning. People come to me and say, "I have a teenager who is acting out. What can I do?" I say to them, "Start watering the tree."

B iblical precepts can be positive or negative, and there is no hierarchy that defines which one is more important than the other. There is no assigned consequence when we break a particular precept. Why is this? Why can a man who keeps the precepts still suffer, while another who fails to keep them does not suffer in the same way? The answer is that each of us has done different things throughout our many lifetimes, and the consequences of our actions are dependent on the work that we were sent here to do. Sometimes a person comes back to make only a small correction; that soul might simply need to come through the birth canal and then it can leave. But we need to understand that the corrections each of us is here to make are different for everyone.

oor means only one thing—the absence of Light. He who is poor lacks that Divine essence that gives him the desire and the striving to exist.

here is no cure for tetanus, diphtheria, whooping cough, or polio. But there is a way we can prevent ourselves from getting these diseases in the first place—it's called inoculation. Spiritual work is our inoculation against darkness and negativity.

ometimes when a person decides to get closer to the Creator, he finds that every-thing in his life changes. He loses friends; he loses money; everything seems to go wrong. The reason this happens is that when we embark on a spir-itual path, we have to start shedding those things that hold us back. Maybe the money we had in our lives didn't come to us in a completely pure way. Or maybe a friend we had wasn't really a true friend. When these things are "taken" from us, we think that we are being punished or we wonder why we are being made to suffer so. We forget that the so-called suffering we are experiencing is because of previous choices we have made—it is not from the Creator.

When it comes to prayer, especially prayer within the confines of a place of worship of any kind, it is important that we keep our thoughts and our focus on spiritual concepts. This is so the angels can take the energy and direct it where it needs to go. If we allow our minds to wander, the angels are unable to do their job.

The best way to prevent a tree from becoming diseased is by taking proper care of it from the moment the seed is placed in the ground. We are like trees, and if we don't start with strong roots, we'll have to do a lot of soul searching and spiritual work to grow properly towards the Light. But this is what the Creator expects of us. He asks that we transform ourselves and share the shade of our strong branches with those around us.

We can learn a great deal from Joseph the Righteous. Although Joseph was surrounded by darkness, he always chose the Light. We, too, must try to look at the Light side of all that appears negative in our life.

ost of us today are not free. We are slaves to our jobs, to our families, and to our worldly responsibilities. I'm not saying that we shouldn't work. Most people have to work, but how much of our work are we doing with love in our hearts? Too often, people work for 50 years, only to find that at the end of the road, they aren't any further along than they were at the beginning. They say, "I'm working to support my family." But they hardly even know their family. This is slavery.

ou cannot bring about kindness, goodness, and peace with hatred and bombs. The only way you can bring about kindness, goodness, and peace is with the Light. After studying spirituality, children in the Middle East are now saying, "I didn't know that we could play together. I thought we were only supposed to fear one another." If we can transform hatred to kindness with the children of the Middle East, we should certainly be able to do so anywhere in the world.

If you don't have the ability to go beyond yourself and to sit for a moment in peaceful silence, then you cannot appreciate who and what you really are. You are a spark of the Lightforce of God. Still your mind—this is how you learn to appreciate.

Without the quality of sharing, there really isn't any existence, for existence is only for the purpose of giving to humanity. When you give to humanity, it will give back to you.

Freedom is being able to do what you enjoy, whether or not you make money at it. You are driven to do it because it is your life's work.

hy are Shekhem and Hebron always the center of such negativity? These two cities were ruled by the Levites, who were the essence of judgment. Within the safety of the Temple, the Levites performed songs of praise to draw down the energy of the Lightforce of the Creator and used this to judge with a balanced hand. It is said that the Levites were made to cut off their hair because hair is an antenna to receive energy. In the Temple and with their hair removed, the Levites could manage this energy of judgment. They were able to perform their service without bias. But unlike the Levites in the Temple, the Levites of Shekhem and Hebron could not curb the energy, and instead they allowed negativity to rule their choices.

When people create negative energy or positive energy in a place, that energy remains there. If there is negative energy in a city or location, problems will persist in that location, and that is what happened in Shekhem and Hebron. The negativity that caused the disregard of the Light, bred more negativity and darkness. This is an important lesson for us to understand.

hildren are in an alpha state until the age of 12, so they do not have the veils that we as adults have. In fact, we veil our own children. Adults, on the other hand, function on the beta level, which is why it's sometimes difficult for children and adults to communicate effectively with one another.

However, when we raise our eyes slightly, the brain automatically triggers an alpha level. So if you want to reach your children, sit with them at night or early in the morning, lift your eyes so you're on an alpha level, too, and give them all the positive thoughts and images you want their personalities to develop and understand. Tell them, "I love you. You are a good person." When you do this, you're feeding their souls at the alpha level.

In alpha, there is no judgment. It is like flying in an airplane. Once you go above the clouds, there is only calm.

very part of our body is affected by our thoughts and by the energy of the food we eat. The body is strong when the mind is positive and at ease. When we follow a negative thought with a negative action, we cause a flaw in our body's functioning. We become weak. And when we become weak, we cause dis-ease in our body.

The science of kinesiology demonstrates this well. Kinesiology is a system that uses muscle testing to identify areas of weakness in the body. For instance, our muscles respond quite differently to "I love you" than to "I hate you."

The people who get sick the most often—and I'm not talking here about the minor colds that everyone gets—are those people who have the most negative mental framework. If we have negative thoughts, our body becomes weak. When we maintain positive thoughts, our body remains strong.

hose who read the Bible know that the sun and moon were created on the Fourth Day. On this day, there was an argument in the cosmos. The Moon said that it wanted the same light as the Sun, but the Light said that there could not be two kings under one crown. The Moon represents *Malkhut* and the Sun, *Zeir Anpin*. As we know in this physical world, the moon has no light of its own, but rather it receives its light from the sun. Like the moon, we in the level of *Malkhut,* have no Light of our own. We receive our Light through the spiritual work that we do that reveals the Light in our physical dimension.

Moses represents the Light of *Zeir Anpin*, which is the light of the sun, and the Promised Land represents the Vessel, or the moon. Moses could not enter the Promised Land until the work of the Vessel to transform itself from the *Desire to Receive* to the *Desire to Share* was complete. God said that Moses could not enter because it was too soon for the Messiah, the time when the Light in its totality will be revealed. It was not yet time.

But the time is coming. When the light of the moon becomes equal to the light of the sun, it will signal that the work of the Vessel is complete.

ow often do we ask, "What is it that I can do to create something more pleasant and beautiful in my life?" The answer lies in our friends and the people with whom we share our environment. They help create our frame of mind. This is the Universal Law of Cause and Effect at work. If you want to something pleasant and beautiful, look to the people you allow into your life.

n the presence of the Light, everyone is equal—separation does not exist. There is no differentiation between Muslims, Christians, Jews, and any other faith. When we talk of the Light, we are talking about a unity that bypasses all differences. There are four known blood types, but no type contains a racial or religious code. Each of us contains only a universal blood code. In this way, we are united as One.

A spiritual person is someone who says, "This is who I am. If you like what I have become, then learn from what you see so that you, too, can become a part of the same Light that I am a part of."

Some people have lots of money and material things but are still unhappy. In fact, they seem to be cursed by their material wealth. They are always concerned about how to keep their money, who might want to take their money, and whether they will have enough money. Then there are people who have little material wealth but seem to lead a blessed life. What determines whether something will be a blessing or a curse in our lives is our consciousness.

hose of us who are familiar with natural cures like homeopathy and acupuncture know that prior to a person becoming cleansed or detoxified, they experience what is known as a healing crisis. A healing crisis is when the whole system shuts down and every sickness that you've ever had in your life bombards your body all at once. In other words, you're sick as a dog. But this removal of sickness and negativity is required if your body is to heal.

In the same way, a person who is becoming spiritual goes through a healing crisis in every area of their life. That's the price one pays to become more elevated in consciousness. It's like someone who wants to have a beautiful body. You must exercise. You must exert yourself physically, and it's hard work.

Spirituality is the same way. People aren't born spiritual; they are born only with the potential to become spiritual. Now some people might be born with spiritual gifts, perhaps a gift of clairvoyance or intuition. These gifts do not make a person spiritual; they are simply gifts a person can choose to use. But becoming spiritual requires effort.

O n the Day of Reckoning, the Creator takes into account all that a person has done, negative or positive, as well as that which he will do. There are many people who will enjoy a longer life because of the actions that they have yet to take. We never really know when an action in front of us is the one action that we came here to do. Sometimes we are so busy living life that we forget that with one word, we can change the day or the life of someone else.

P eople generate energy through their thoughts and actions. This cumulative energy can manifest in different ways. A plague is an accumulation of negative actions.

I t is said that it takes 36 people to keep the world going. How many people does it take to destroy it?

simple *light*

I would like to say thank you to the Creator for allowing us to come together and for giving us permission to have this knowledge and this spirituality for all of us to share. I would also like to thank those of you who have come so far to do so much, not just for yourselves but for all the people of the world.

The Kabbalah Centre began with nothing but two people and a shoestring. From these two people, it grew and grew. Now we look at all of our students and ask, "Where did this all come from?" Like a bumblebee that should not be able to fly with its heavy body and small wings, the Kabbalah Centre should not have been able to take flight. But we did, and we have much work before us to do.

n the Story of Pinchas, it was foretold that the women of the Golden Calf would return to rebel against male domination. This is happening as we speak. Today, we see women as chairpeople of large corporations. The woman's voice has become more powerful than ever before in history, and when the female voice becomes this strong, the level of the *Sefira* of *Malkhut* is reached, at which point male and female become equal.

For people born under the astrological sign of Pisces, life is all about hidden emotions and thoughts. These things, which other signs may find easy to deal with, are difficult for a Pisces. A Pisces can be burning up on the inside, and yet their demeanor remains very calm.

Therefore, within the month of Pisces, it is important for us to watch out for subterfuge and hidden enemies. Pisces is a strong sign for business and intellectual pursuits. The spiritual work of the individual Pisces, however, is to learn to cope with their true emotions.

Those who are born under the sign of Pisces often have problems with addiction. When they are unable to deal with their emotions, they tend to hide themselves and cover up those difficult feelings with drugs and alcohol. Because they deny their emotions, they have a lot of pent-up anger.

There's a not-so-funny example that explains the nature of a Pisces. If you tell any other sign that someone went on a killing spree in four states, they would normally answer, "What!? How terrible!" The Pisces, on the other hand, would respond by saying, "Which four states?" This is a testament to the mindset of somebody who has a great deal of Pisces in his chart.

As we grow spiritually, we must never forget the bonds that tie us together. Those bonds—the things we do together—are important not only for the group we are a part of, but also for those outside the group, as well. This is what creates a circuitry of energy.

wo people bless their food before they eat. What's the difference between these two individuals? One says the blessing so that he may eat, while the other desires to eat so that he can say the blessing to thank God. When we live in the consciousness of gratitude and view every day as a Divine gift, the movie of our life becomes filled with miracles.

he *Zohar* says that if you are in a negative place, you will eventually fall into negativity, no matter how righteous you are. At a party where there is cocaine, alcohol, and the like, then as good as your intentions might be, you will be affected by the negativity of the crowd around you.

If we are exposed to negativity for long periods of time, holes form in our aura. When there are enough holes, disease has a space through which to enter.

Even the most righteous can fall into a place of negativity and allow it to become their way of life. But no matter how far you fall into negativity, there is always a way out.

hen a person feels fear, the feeling comes from the cerebellum, the lower part of the brain and the part responsible for our most instinctual responses. So how can we learn to overcome fear? How do we stop the flow of adrenaline that starts charging through our bodies?

Here's one tool I can give you. Write down what you think you're afraid of and then assign a color to it. Chances are your fear-color will be black or red because these are considered negative colors. Now I would like you to ask yourself, "What color would help me to heal this fear?" Visualize the first color that comes to your mind. This will be your healing-color.

Now breathe in your healing-color, at the same time breathing out the color of your fear. Feel your body filling with the energy of healing. Now ask your healing-color to help you locate the seed of your fear because the thing that you *think* you *fear*, is *not* what you're really afraid of. There is something beneath your fear. You need to find the seed—the real cause of that which you fear.

Maybe your real fear is loss of control or a fear of not being loved. Meditate on your healing-color and allow it to reveal the seed of your real fear and the location of this seed in your body.

Once you have done this, I'd like you to write what you discovered on a piece of paper. Whatever it was that came up for you, write that down. Now take a match and burn it. Allow the fire to cleanse you of this fear. As you watch the paper burn, know that you are setting the seed of your fear free for good.

ne of the greatest gifts we have is what nature gives us. We need to take the time to appreciate the great wonder that is there. If we forget, then it becomes much harder to connect to the Light of the Creator.

We receive the greatest Light, not by doing positive actions all our lives but by taking the negative that we have and transforming it into the beauty of life.

The Israelites in the desert were indeed very high souls. They had everything they needed; Korah could even see into the future. But despite having everything, these people still wanted to stone Moses and Aaron.

Moses could not understand why. He bowed down before God and said, "What have I done?" To which God replied, "You have done nothing!"

But there were consequences of the rebellion against Moses. The Earth opened and swallowed Korah and his 250 followers. They lost everything! Their homes and even those things that they had loaned to others were destroyed.

No one could have fathomed why Korah and his followers would do what they did to Moses. How could they possibly think like that after having received so much? What beliefs or thought processes have turned *you* into something that you never thought you would become?

Most of us today think like Kora<u>h</u>. We carry with us a sense of entitlement. We think, "What have *you* done for *me* lately?" After receiving so much, we tend to forget what we have and where we came from. Remember and appreciate!

I t is important to understand that life in this physical dimension is a constant battle. Even the act of coming out of the womb into this world is a battle for both mother and child. However, the battle is not between ourselves and others but between our self and our own ego.

Y ou don't need to pore over the Bible, memorizing the entire story. If you can take one sentence and it sings to you, that is the most important thing.

isease in all its forms manifests when the protective aura around our bodies is weakened through our reactive behavior. Happy people are resistant to disease because they are not involved in depression and anger. Why do they stand a better chance of not being sick? Because they have a different consciousness and therefore treat others differently.

Anger. Greed. I want. I need. What about me? That constant thought of "me, me, me" causes a puncture in our protective shield. Selfish thoughts, actions, and deeds act as a sharp pin to puncture our personal aura, and in a global sense, the ozone layer, which is designed to protect us all.

There is a direct connection between the environment and us. The more that we disrespect nature, the more it regurgitates this toxic state back at us. Even our seemingly most insignificant negative thoughts will affect the world later, even if they don't have an immediate effect. We have been gifted with the knowledge and spiritual ability to alter the chaos that surrounds us. We can change this lack of balance of the Lightforce of God, starting now. Change may begin with only a few thousand people, but it translates to millions if we all use the tools. There is a tremendous amount of Light at our disposal, so we can change the toxicity that exists in our environment into Light, beginning today.

I t's our job to share knowledge with those who have a little less of it, and to learn what we can from those who have a little more. We are here to give as much as we can.

S o often in our lives, our inner voice—our angel of God—will instruct us not to take a particular action because of the negative outcome that will follow if we do. But when we are led by Ego, we figure out all the reasons why we should ignore the angelic voice and do what we want to do anyway. We need to learn to weigh our actions by asking, "How is this action going to affect others? If I take this action, am I being considerate of the entire human race?" These questions can act as guidelines for all our behavior.

veryone has a problem in some area of his or her life. In that same place is the hole that needs to be sealed in this incarnation. This is our correction—to close up the opening of that hole so that Satan can't enter.

This is what takes place on the *Ninth of Av*. On this day, the hole—ultimately our correction—is revealed. Closing up this hole is our personal Messiah, our personal perfection. It's easy for us to see another person's problems and faults. But that's not why we are here. Our correction is to seek out, to see, and to contemplate our *own* problem—the hole *we* made, the one we have to fix—and not to criticize and judge others.

here can the most Light be revealed? In someone who has grown up righteous from birth or in someone who has a lot of negativity? The answer is in the person who has the most negativity. We can take this lesson into our daily lives by transforming our lowest point of negativity into the highest level of spirituality.

When a great Light is to come into the world, it often manifests in the dirtiest, lowliest Vessel. If it originated from a righteous place, there would be no opportunity for transformation. So what does the Creator do? He puts His Light in the dirtiest Vessel! So shine up your Vessel and let the Light shine.

hat does a name mean? A name is energy. When Adam was told to name the animals, he didn't just decide on a whim that a horse should be called a horse. No, it was the energy of the animal itself that created the name "horse."

I t is said that in every generation, there are 36 righteous people who hold up the world. These individuals remain concealed to us, but they are the pillars that are essential for keeping the world in balance. It is also said that there are certain righteous people, each of whom is the equivalent of 100,000 individuals. This illustrates that no one ever knows how much energy one powerful soul is worth in the game of the Universe—just as when we throw a rock into the water, we never really know the full effect of the ripples we create.

We do know, however, that when we do something positive, we create a positive result, even though this might not be immediately apparent. So many people say to me, "I study spirituality, I share, I volunteer, so how come my life isn't wonderful? How come I'm not married or how come I am married but don't want to be? So many "How comes?!" The answer is that Kabbalah gives us tools, which allow us to live a better way of life. This doesn't mean, however, that we will no longer experience the hassles of life; in fact, it's just the opposite—the closer you become to the Light, the more difficult the path often becomes.

Think of it this way. When we decide to lose weight, what do we do? We go to a gym and work up a sweat. No pain, no gain, right? But when it comes to our spiritual health, we just want it to be easy. But that is not how it works. The higher we climb on the ladder, the more difficult life becomes. In fact, we see more negativity than ever before. This is because before we began our spiritual journey, we didn't really notice the negative things that were all around us. But when we become attuned and connect to a higher energy, we see so much more. Friends or partners might leave us either because they're not on the same path as we are or because they don't relate to us anymore.

Things change. Just remember that every time a door closes, another one opens to allow new energy to come into our lives. There will be a return on our investment, even if we don't see it right away. Sometimes just having this understanding can make a great difference in people's lives.

No, our lives will not become a bed of roses because we have decided to read spiritual teachings. But we can learn to appreciate the negative things that happen in our lives recognizing them as opportunities from which to learn and grow. I know many people who became spiritual because of adversities like disease or separation in their lives, and these people have come to grow and become better human beings because of those situations. This is the power of walking a spiritual path—we just have to be patient enough to reap the rewards.

The *Zohar* asks: "How does one know if a person is truly united with God and with his own spirituality?" You'll know because this person will be quiet; this is because a truly spiritual person speaks less and does more.

nce upon a time, there was a student who came to his teacher and said to him, "How can I study the Bible all day. I need to work to bring home bread." His teacher turned to him and said, "Yes, it says that you should study all day. When at work, if a customer asks for a pound of grain, then provide a just measurement. That is the Bible. When someone asks to borrow money, loan that person money in a way that is fair. That is the Bible. Make the money that you need to live, but no more. That is the Bible. In this way, you are a student of the Bible all day long."

isharmony need not exist. If something happens to you—if you are in an uncomfortable situation—try to turn it around, not just in your moments of discomfort but at all times. Each and every one of us has the power to prevent wars and natural disasters. We are all part of the Light energy, and we all have the power to change that which is dark into Light.

This is what it means to be spiritual. We need to use the tools available to us—from whatever spiritual path we are on and from whatever our course of study—to advance the cause of unity, not separation; the cause of human dignity; and the cause of respectful treatment for our fellow beings. We are all a part of this purpose.

The most powerful prayers, *Kol Nidrei*, *Kaddish*, *Berikh Shemei*, are all in Aramaic. This is because the angels do not understand the language of Aramaic. If they were to understand our prayers, they would interfere in our process. But when we pray to God in Aramaic without interference or support from an angel, we are saying in essence, "I know that I do not deserve Your Light, but I am standing before You nevertheless and asking that in Your great compassion, You will give Your Light to me."

Most of us know we can't learn to fly an airplane by listening to lectures or reading through diagrams. It's the same with spirituality. We cannot become spiritual by meditating or simply studying. Knowledge that is kept inside and not shared or acted upon will remain just that—knowledge. Spirituality is not what we *learn*, but the way we *use what we learn* in our daily life.

e all judge, but passing judgment in our present state—with all of the veils that are covering us—prevents us from genuinely helping others. If a person is talking to me, but I don't really listen because I think I already know where they are coming from, then it is impossible for me to help. I have already acted as judge and jury! So we must step outside of ourselves, our opinions, and the veils that cover us before we can really understand another and offer our help.

cience says that the immune system is everything, so what makes the immune system strong and able to fight disease? The answer is happiness and balance. Happy people are content with who they are and where they are.

When we look at others and feel jealous of what we feel they have and we lack, we create an empty space, a hole in our personal and global ozone layer. Every time we feel jealous of another, we perforate the vibrating energy that protects us. And when there are enough holes, disease can enter.

arai and Abram could not conceive a child, but when their names were changed to Sarah and Abraham, she was able to give birth to Isaac. The names Sarai and Sarah and Abram and Abraham represent the inner and outer worlds. With the addition of the Hebrew letter *Hei* to both their names, they were able to achieve a higher consciousness and bring a child into the world. The names we are given affect the energy frequency we draw into our lives and how we vibrate with them.

eel the energy of the person next to you and treat him as you yourself would like to be treated. To be able to look at another and offer love instead of judgment is the greatest restriction *and* the greatest level of a spiritual being. All of us have times of judgment, but when we treat others with respect and love, we can transform that judgment into mercy.

*m*any may not realize this, but it was only 35 years ago when the technology and wisdom of Kabbalah were made available to the masses. Before then, people did not know of Rav Shimon bar Yochai or the *Zohar*. But because of the dedication and energy of the tens of thousands of people who desired to study and share this wisdom, we are reaching out to the world. People will receive this knowledge at whatever level they are at: There is no right or wrong with these levels, only a difference in the level of receiving. Some will understand and make use of only a little, while others will understand and make use of more.

What is important is that because of people's participation, the entire world is becoming aware that there is a choice. Information exists that will enable us to eliminate pain and suffering and improve our own lives and the lives of others. If we hesitate to share this knowledge and the existence of Kabbalah with others because we are afraid of what they might say or think, then we leave them unaware of the tools that are available to them.

ho is the person who gets robbed? It's the person who's afraid of being robbed. Who gets mugged? The person who's afraid of being mugged. Who is the person who's a victim of failed relationships? It's the person who expects to be hurt. Why?

Our thoughts create our reality. If we say, "Oh God, if I go out this late, somebody might attack me," what type of energy are we connecting to? Negative energy. And that negative energy vibrates. The people who suffer the most from painful situations in life are people who are afraid of these very situations.

Now I'm *not* saying that we should leave our doors open and our cars unlocked. What I *am* saying, however, is that when one thinks a negative thought, he is expressing doubt in the Creator. This creates an empty space in the cosmic realm—and that empty space is filled with negativity. Therefore, those who are most often victims of negativity are people who have created it for themselves.

here is a story of an old man who comes to his spiritual teacher and says, "I have tried to live a spiritual life by running away from honor and respect. Now I am a very old man, but I have yet to receive any honor or respect for all I have done." His teacher asked, "While you were running, how often did you look back to see if it was running after you?"

Spirituality is not something you "get" because you've shown up; nor is it something that comes just because you have simply participated in it.

We must be willing to suffer for spirituality, to work for it, and most of all, to understand that the person next to us is just as important as we are. We are all sparks of the same Light, and we have all come here for the same collective purpose—to remove chaos from this world. This is our job, and this is how we earn our honor.

If a person says that they believe in God, it means that they doubt the existence of God. This is because "believing" is not the same as "knowing." Knowing something with certainty is what creates the connection to the Light; while beliefs only create chaos, disconnection, and doubt.

Although the candle flickers, the nature of the light it creates never changes. As the wick burns, only the wax melts; the light remains. In the same way, the Light that we give to others close to us remains long after the wax of the candle—our body—is gone, for the Light of God is infinite.

veryone can learn to see auras. First, you see the energy that surrounds a person, usually foremost around the head. If you see only a small emanation, it means that the person is tired or sick. A broken aura or one with gaps in it means that the person's energy is not flowing properly due to a blockage somewhere in the body. It can also mean that the person is closed off to new ideas.

Everything has an aura. Kirlian photography shows the energy in trees and plants as well as in people. It's also important to note that when you lie or react negatively, your aura changes to reflect this negative vibration. A person's aura can reveal a great deal about their spiritual and physical existence.

hen Moses came down from Mount Sinai after the Revelation of the Ten Utterances, the people were not yet ready to receive the Light that the Creator wanted to give them. Therefore, Moses had to go back up the mountain for another 40 days and nights before coming down again.

Let's hope that when that Light comes into our lives, we are there to say that our Vessels are prepared to receive it in the manner in which it is to be received.

eople ask why must there be negativity? Because only through the transformation of our personal negativity can we become full of Light.

rue strength is brought about only by nurturing it, by working for it, and by being a part of it. We should all work to generate true strength, not only for ourselves but for everyone on Earth, so that each one of us becomes a beacon of Light. Let our effort bring about so much energy for those whom we love and for those who love us, that it spills over to all the peoples of the world. Let us pray that through our work, we will bring about immortality for all humanity.

he month of Capricorn, governed by the planet Saturn, is called "Old Father Time." Old Father Time gives only as much as we are willing to work for. In the month of Capricorn, there are no gifts—there is only hard work. As the steady goat climbs the mountain, so does the Capricorn. The ability for us to change our nature and to trust the outside world is difficult and will take a lot of time and effort to achieve. But the reward is great!

When a place is left vacant or a person dies, the soul departs the Vessel, leaving an emptiness behind. The force that enters this void is negative, and this negativity can affect all of the surrounding area. If someone dies at home, the negativity affects the whole house until that house is cleansed of it.

The Tabernacle was built by Betsalel and Ohaliav. The *Zohar* says that when Betsalel was about to begin, he went to God and asked, "Who am I to be a part of the building of Your House? Why have you chosen me?" The reason he was chosen was because of his willingness—because he said to God, "These are my hands. Use them to do Your work." And the entire building of the Tabernacle was made his.

ost of us have fears. We fear death because we know that we haven't finished what we came here to do and we won't have an opportunity to take that action or make that correction.

We have unfounded fears—a fear of flying or a fear of heights, for example. We also have founded fears. A founded fear is something based on a direct experience in this lifetime, such as being bitten by a dog. But even the dog bite occurred to teach us a lesson because of something that we did to someone else or some injustice that we caused.

So in essence, all of our fears, nightmares, and anxieties come from a Cause that is not given to us in this lifetime. They represent a barrier that we must overcome in order to fulfill our purpose.

*L*ove is hard work. It is not simple *to be loved*, nor is it simple *to love*. To love, we must understand that the Light of God is both mine and yours. We can't steal another's Light. The only right we have is to share our own earned Light. That's what we are striving for.

*T*he Bible often refers to idol worship. What is idol worship? Idol worship occurs when a person ignores or even denies the influence of the Creator in his or her success. This person falsely believes that their efforts alone were the cause of their achievements. This is what idol worship is really about. Perhaps when we view it in this way, we can see how idol worship might at times play a role in our own lives.

ach and every one of us can take the Light and create a circle of protection. The Light, the tools, and the technology are the only weapons we have to use against the darkness. We have to be careful of how we act—it is our actions that tell the darkness whether to leave or to stay. Let us not hurt those closest to us; instead, let our actions create a bond of oneness. Only through an accumulation of spiritual enlightenment can we clothe ourselves in a protective shield.

nstead of feeling doubt every time something seemingly negative happens, what we should say is, "I don't understand this situation, but I've done everything that I can to make it a positive experience. So I'll have certainty that in the larger scheme of things, this situation is indeed positive." With this consciousness, we give darkness no entry into our situation.

here is a story that the Levites, who while taking the Tabernacle from place to place, were dying one by one. The problem was that their thoughts were not of total certainty. And since they were dealing with direct Light, there was no room for doubt, so they immediately disintegrated.

Like the thoughts of the Levites, our thoughts and emotions also manifest themselves physically. This applies to both positive and negative thoughts and feelings. Even something as insignificant as a smile or frown creates a physical response inside the body. We have to remember this and share of ourselves more often and with more intention, realizing what is happening on a physical level when we do.

piritual people know that, before they leave this world, they need to accomplish what they came here to do. The reason many people fear death is because deep down inside, they know they have not yet completed what they came here to accomplish.

I t's not up to us to decide what a person's spiritual level is or what they can or cannot do. This is because a person can transform all of his negativity and lack of spirituality with one small act of kindness. In that one act of generosity, everything can be turned around. The greatest act is transforming our *Desire to Receive for the Self Alone* into a *Desire to Receive for the Sake of Sharing*, and everyone has the ability to perform this act.

K abbalah teaches that to have balance, we need to connect to the Three-Column System of Right, Left, and Central Columns. Sometimes the idea of balance is very difficult because, although we are part of Creation and have the Light of God within us, our insecurities and feelings of inferiority get in the way. They cause us to move away from the Creator's great intentions for us because we feel unworthy of attaining those goals. When we find ourselves with this mindset, we must share our Light and that will bring us balance.

emember, the garment that we each have been given—the body that each of us has—was created so that we would be able to make our correction in that form. But let's not ever forget that our body is only a garment—we connect to the Lightforce only through the beauty of our soul. The closer we can get to this Light energy, the more beautiful and whole our entire Universe becomes. There's no such thing as evil, only a lack of Light. Overcoming that lack of Light for the benefit of all mankind is our job—yours and mine.

When we are in a half-sleep state, our mind is very much open and susceptible to outside stimuli and messages.

Under anesthesia, a patient—although he or she may look asleep—has a subconscious mind that is very much awake. This means that when a healthcare worker uses positive words and messages in the operating room, it can have a marked effect on the patient's experience and recovery.

In this way, science is demonstrating what Kabbalah has known for thousands of years—that the state of one's consciousness greatly affects that person's physical state.

We can use this same knowledge and technique to effect change in our daily lives. Try this tool the next time you awaken from slumber. During your state of half-awakedness, set a positive intention for the day. Ask God where it is that you are meant to reveal Light during the next 24 hours and how you can create harmony. By doing this, you are "programming" your subconscious to be open to any opportunity to share Light with the world.

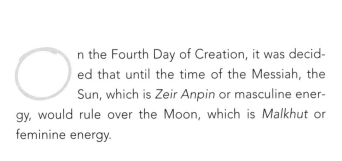

On the Fourth Day of Creation, it was decided that until the time of the Messiah, the Sun, which is *Zeir Anpin* or masculine energy, would rule over the Moon, which is *Malkhut* or feminine energy.

When we understand this, we can better understand why, throughout history, the female has been oppressed. Within the context of the Bible, we see that the struggle by women throughout the generations existed because it was not yet time for the Lightforce of the female to shine equal to the Light of her male counterpart.

But now during the Age of Aquarius—a time of serious depletion of spiritual energy—the female is rising to the occasion, and the Sun and the Moon will soon have equal Light.

hen we are in fear, we are no longer con-nected to the positive energy of the Light. When we're in fear, it's the "I" that's afraid. It's the "I" that doesn't want to feel pain or loss. But when we are connected to the Light, there is no "I" or "me" or Ego. When we eliminate Ego, we eliminate fear.

et's try to remember to be happy for the many blessings that we so often forget about. Remember the "Thank you" you forgot to say, the letter you should have written, the friend who just needed to feel your arms around him or her for a moment? These forgotten actions—all of these small kindnesses we didn't take the time to do—are the things that bother us at night when we are alone. Let us pray that tomorrow we can all sleep peacefully because we haven't forgotten the humani-ty that makes us all One.

There is a story about a great sage and his congregation who prayed and prayed on one of the holiest days of the year. Despite their prayers, they were denied entry into the Upper Worlds. At the end of the day, the sage cried out to God, "I don't know what more to do. Many of us here have sins hanging over our heads? What can we do to change our destinies?"

Before God could respond, there appeared a small child who wanted so much to please God but couldn't speak. So he took a harmonica and started to play with all his heart and all his might. The people around him began to complain, "How dare he play this music? How can he disturb this silent prayer? Doesn't he know we are trying to open the Heavenly Gates?" Suddenly the sage said, "Be quiet and stop complaining. The Gates to the Upper Worlds are opening!"

It is not our ability to say the prayer or the way we sound when we pray that is important. Rather, what is important is the desire we bring to our prayers that will open up the Gates to the Upper World—not only for ourselves, but for everyone.

he reason we experience anxiety is because we are always playing a game— according to Kabbalah, that game is the Game of Life. The players are humanity in the form of their "I, my, me" Ego. Most of our anxiety dwells in thoughts like "Who am I and what am I and what will happen to me when this or that occurs?"

For instance, we worry about our children. We worry because they are *our* children, after all. And therefore, if they don't come home on time or if they're sick, we worry. We worry about them because they are part of us. Please, don't misunderstand me. I'm not saying that it's wrong to have concern. But it's important to realize that our anxiety about our children is connected to our *Desire to Receive for the Self Alone*. If we truly understood the role the Light plays in our lives, we wouldn't have any anxiety. We would know that whatever circumstances appear in our life—regarding our children or anything else for that matter—they are there to teach us lessons that we are meant to learn.

The reason that Moses was chosen to be the leader of Israel was because he was humble, he was pure, and he genuinely believed that he was nobody special.

Something drives us to be more spiritual. Whatever it is that makes our consciousness more aware of our spiritual being, does not happen by accident. It happens because we have finally reached the level where our soul is yearning for spiritual nourishment. A book, a friend, a "coincidence"—all can bring us to the place our soul was meant to be. Once we are on the path, it is up to us to decide what we will do with this new awareness. The end of the path is known, but we decide how long it will take and how hard it will be for us to get there.

e think sometimes that we are so great, but we are only dust. We are nothing but a vehicle to bring the Lightforce of God closer to ourselves and to the rest of the world. If we think we are more than that, we're wrong.

f we are of the right consciousness, whatever comes to us will be ours. This is because we'll be able to take any negativity that comes our way and transform it into Light. If we constantly draw in negative energy without transforming it, we cannot achieve our proper *Tikkun*, or spiritual correction.

t this time in history, the world is full of many old souls who know that a spiritual awakening is in the works.

I f you plan on humbly advising somebody else on what to do, make sure that you are coming from a place of love and that they are willing to listen. If you love them but know they aren't willing to listen, your advice will fall on deaf ears. And if you are not coming from a place of love, then you are offering advice out of Ego, and no Light can come from this.

E very person has their own road to take in this life; we can't take it for them.

I n Kabbalah, we learn that we can't coerce someone into spirituality. The best way to bring somebody to a higher awareness is to demonstrate to that person our own growth, how we have changed, and what we have become. This is how we guide someone onto a spiritual path—not by saying, "You should do this" or "You should do that." This does not foster real growth. And sometimes we have to step away from the person so that they are allowed to fall and then pick themselves up. This is how we all learn and grow.

We need to look at the negative emotions that wreak havoc with our lives. For instance, jealousy is the inability to appreciate what we have. When we feel we lack something, we create jealousy. But if we can identify the negative emotions we have, we can work on transforming them into the opposite of what they represent. We can turn a feeling of lack into a feeling of abundance and, in the process, gain unity with our spirit.

We cannot afford to give energy to these negative emotions. Any negative emotion creates a black hole, thus making us susceptible to disease. There isn't any physical cure for spitefulness or hatred. All we can do is admit to ourself, "I have this negative quality, and this is what I have to do to correct it."

pirituality is believing that everyone has the right to draw spiritual energy and to bring that Light into their lives and the lives of others. It's being cognizant that this Lightforce transcends the physical world and exists in each and every person. It's about caring for the welfare of others and not just looking out for ourselves. When this is our spirituality, we can arrive at a place where we have a sense of unity with our neighbor and the blessing of the Light in our lives and in the world.

ithin the 72 Names of God, there is only one letter that is missing, and that is *Gimel*. This is because the *Gimel* represents *ge'ava*, or "pride." Pride overrides a person's awareness and appreciation of the Light in their life.

There are many people who must struggle for success but manage to make something of themselves, just as there are many who struggle but fail to achieve success. What is the difference between these two types of people? They both have the potential of the Creator within, but one desires success so that he can share it with others, while the other desires success only so he can feel good about himself.

We have a choice—either to be a Light for the world or to be a Light only for ourselves. On our path to success, there must be the recognition that only the power of the Light will allow us to fulfill our purpose. If we are following a higher purpose that is supported by the Light, then we will succeed.

A n angel's power is strictly limited to the particular job it was created to perform. There isn't a blade of grass that grows that does not have an angel looking over it. In the same way, we each have our own job—a specific purpose for which we came into this world—and it is within that realm that we must function.

I t is said in the *Zohar* that the Final Redemption will come when we have reached a critical mass. Reaching this critical mass is not dependent on a specific number of people; it is dependent on whether each person is performing the particular job he or she was put on the Earth to do.

A person never knows how much Light they reveal in the world by giving of their energy to someone else.

In the eyes of the Creator, today, yesterday, and tomorrow are all an illusion. Time exists only in our physical world.

There are many women who are married to men who are not as spiritually evolved as they are. These women can choose to leave their husbands or they can choose to make their partners believe they are spiritually effective. The best way to help your partner to elevate spiritually is by being an example of the spiritual principles that you embody.

The female is a Vessel to contain the Light of God—a Vessel that manifests the Lightforce of the Creator by taking the energy she has received from the male and elevating it to a place where the male can grow spiritually and be nourished.

As we come closer and closer to the Final Redemption, we will experience a time of great destruction, but it will also be a time of great construction and revelation of Light. The *Zohar* says that at that time, there will be people who will fight to better themselves and this world.

Let us not wait for a tragedy to wake us up and prompt us to fight. Let us remember to appreciate what this life is about and not be left saying, "This is what I should have done" or "I should have said 'I love you' to those around me." We should not take those whom we love for granted because we never know when the opportunity to share our Light with them will be gone.

We have a great deal of negativity inside of us, so much that it's an innate condition of human beings to see a glass as half empty. However, the one thing we can do to turn that response around is to resist those negative thoughts and urges. When we restrict our negativity, it generates a more powerful level of Light. In fact, the one who gets closest to the Lightforce is not the one who is passive but the one who is able to convert their negativity into positive energy.

We must remember that the reason we exist is because the Light inside us is yearning to return to where it belongs. It's up to us to bring it closer to the Godhead. This can only happen when we remove our *Desire to Receive for Self Alone* and transform it.

ngels are created by the words that pass our lips. In other words, when we defame or hurt somebody with our words or when we fail to say kind words, we create negative angels for ourselves. And the opposite is also true—we create positive angels through the sharing of positive words and actions.

oday, with the tools and the wisdom that we have, we are able to transform the chaos that is around us. Not only *can* we do it, but we *must* do it. Not only is it our job to fill ourselves with Light, we also have the ability and the responsibility to transmit the Lightforce of God to others.

In the story of Isaac and Rivka, the Bible tells us that Isaac first knew Rivka, then she became his wife, and then he loved her. Normally, we meet someone, fall in love, and then get married. That's the typical scenario. Why is it that the Bible specifies that Isaac knew Rivka, she became his wife, and then he loved her?

Many people become involved in a relationship mainly for companionship. You enjoy doing things together and you feel comfortable with that other person. So when does it become love? At what point did Isaac and Rivka's relationship become a relationship of love? The answer lies in the Hebrew word for love, ahava.

Ahava is spelled *Alef Hei Bet Hei*. The numerical values of the letters *Alef Hei Bet Hei* add up to 13. The Hebrew word for one, *ehad*, also has the numerical value of 13. So what is *ahava*? What is love? Love is two people functioning as one unified entity. It is the intermingling and the interdependence of two souls.

Most relationships do not function on this level. They function out of emotional need, financial reasons, or a fear of being alone. But a true relationship between souls is one in which one soul complements the other. When one soul is down, the other's strength lifts them up, and vice versa. The two souls function and act as a whole, a complete unit. This is what it means to love, and this is why the Bible explains that the love that existed between Isaac and Rivka was one of unity.

Wealth can become a gold-plated prison if we allow it. If we become a slave to our wealth by sacrificing time with our families, then not only will we be unable to enjoy our riches, but our children will suffer the consequences of our enslavement, as well. The delight of having family, friends, and children around us—this is true wealth. Money and recognition become immaterial when we have the love of those closest to us.

The kabbalists have known for thousands of years that there is another Universe out there—a parallel Universe. While we exist in and observe our physical environment, there is a simultaneously existing Flawless Universe—a Universe that knows nothing of chaos, illness, and suffering.

We are the Vessels of the Lightforce of God. If we allow Him to enter our hearts, we must also be prepared to use that which we have been given to warm the hearts of others.

Remember that you are the most precious thing the Creator has put on this Earth.

People are striving to find their spiritual purpose and to become better human beings. But once we embark on a spiritual path, it can actually become harder for us to figure out what it is that we are meant to do. We think things should come easier to us now that we've found spirituality. We think, "I'm on the path, so why isn't my life perfect yet? Why haven't I made the money I had hoped to make or met the person of my dreams yet?" But who says that you are supposed to accomplish these things at all?

Even if we become spiritual, we shouldn't look to Heaven for a quick fix because a spiritual path doesn't always run straight. In fact, the things we must do on our spiritual path may be far more difficult than anything we might encounter on a "normal" path. This is because, in order to have free will, we must encounter equal measure of darkness and Light. As our Light grows, so does the darkness that will challenge us. But this is what makes the Light that we earn so rewarding. After all, what meaning is there in winning a championship against an inferior team?

One of the lessons of the Bible is that a person might witness a miracle of God today but then turn around tomorrow and say to Him, "What have you done for me lately?" We should ask ourselves, "Where in our lives are we taking the miracles of God for granted?"

In the Temple, there was always sweet-smelling incense. Different fragrances, when inhaled, open up our connection to the Light. For this reason, we should always keep the sweet smell of incense in our home. Let's allow our homes and our hearts to be the rose that brings a sweet fragrance to the world.

All people possess traits that are not to our liking. But we must love the spark of God that resides in each person, and with a breath of kindness, gently blow away those things that we would prefer to judge.

abbi Akiva was one of the greatest souls to ever inhabit the Earth. According to Rav Isaac Luria, the Ari, Rabbi Akiva was from the lineage of Cain. Cain was an envious man who killed his brother, but from the seed of this envious man, Rabbi Akiva would be born into this world. The lesson for us is that the greatest amount of Light will always come from the Negative Side. It is when we are in dirt up to our chins and feel there is no way out that we can reveal the most Light. Like the great soul Rabbi Akiva, whose heritage was imbued with negativity, we can use our darkness to the advantage of the world. This type of profound transformation cannot come from someone who is born of goodness or has done good his entire life. To become a soul like Rabbi Akiva, we have to work for it.

ome may pray all their lives, but their prayers are by rote. It's not about saying the words; it's about becoming the prayer itself.

art of our work in Kabbalah is learning to look ourselves in the eye. We like to figure out what is wrong with the other person—our partner, our neighbor, our co-worker—but we have to remember that when we point a finger at everyone else, there are four fingers pointing back at us!

any times in our life, God sends us a sign. But we are often too consumed by our own problems and desires to heed these signs, which are generally there to warn us of darkness ahead.

he *Zohar* says that at the time of the Temple, a pigeon was a unique sacrifice in that a pigeon represented peace; however, it could not be given as an offering to bring about peace. The only time a pigeon could be given for this purpose was when the person making the offering had achieved a state of peace himself. We understand from this that what is considered an appropriate sacrifice always depends on the person making that sacrifice. For instance, a billionaire could not give $100 as an offering because, for him and for his Vessel, this is no sacrifice at all.

uring a person's birthday month, he or she experiences a great deal of change and transformation. This is because this particular time represents the greatest opportunity to make corrections for the coming year in order to reveal more Light for the world.

The first thing that we learn in Kabbalah is that everything has a purpose and that nothing that happens is random.

The Bible refers to two mountains: one where curses are handed out and one where blessings are bestowed. Sacrifices were performed at the mountain of curses. Why on the mount of curses? Because it is only through sacrifice that Light can be revealed and the mountain of blessings can be reached. Let us work hard to transform darkness into Light and curses into blessings.

When we are on a spiritual path, the Light shows us signs to let us know we are heading in the right direction. It's like flying in an airplane. When we rise above the clouds, the sun is always shining. In the same way, when we rise above those things that cloud our inner Light, the Light is always shining brightly and illuminating our path.

Some 30 years ago, I took the receipts from classes and was going to the bank to deposit them. I was carrying about $1000 in an envelope. On my way, I stopped in a grocery store to pick up some things, but when I came back to the car, the envelope with the money wasn't there. I thought perhaps I had left the envelope back at the office, but it wasn't there either.

I retraced my steps to the grocery store where I saw a number of people milling around. I asked them if they had seen an envelope with $1000, and they said yes, that they had found the envelope and had called the police. The policeman was there and handed me the envelope with the money. I was amazed—I hadn't expected such a thing to happen, that I would get the money back! But it shows us that we should never fear losing those things that are truly ours; if they really belong to us, they can never be taken away. What we really need to look at are those things that we do not want to share and aren't really ours in the first place. Why do we hold onto them so tightly?

e need to ask ourselves: "What did I do today that is different from yesterday?" As long as we still have breath in our bodies, we can change and transform.

rom this day forward, we have the opportunity to change. The only problem is that it's sometimes difficult to discover what it is that we are being called upon to change in ourselves. How do we discover what it is that we need to change? A good place to start is by looking at those places where we get into the most trouble. Maybe it's the way we speak or communicate, what we say or don't say, what we do or don't do. Look closely—the answers are sure to reveal themselves. This discovery process is not to be dreaded; we can undertake it with relish and happiness.

THE KABBALAH CENTRE®

What is Kabbalah?

Kabbalah is the world's oldest body of spiritual wisdom, containing the long-hidden keys to the secrets of the Universe, as well as the keys to the mysteries of the human heart and soul. It's a workable system that allows you to understand your purpose for being here experiencing the joy you were put on Earth to have. In fact, that's what Kabbalah means to receive, to get.

Kabbalah teaches that in order to claim the gifts you were created to receive, you need to earn them by undertaking your spiritual work the process of fundamentally transforming yourself as you climb out of the darkness and into the Light. By helping you recognize the sources of negativity in your own mind and heart, Kabbalah gives you the tools for positive change.

Kabbalistic teachings explain the complexities of the material and the nonmaterial Universe and the physical and metaphysical nature of all humankind.

Moses, Pythagorus, and Sir Isaac Newton are a few of the individuals who studied Kabbalah to understand the spiritual laws of the Universe and their effect on the physical world.

Kabbalah is meant to be used, not merely learned. It can help you remove chaos, pain, and suffering from your life and bring you clarity, understanding, and freedom.

Who Can Study?

Today, millions of people of all faiths have discovered the wisdom and experienced the powerful effects of studying Kabbalah.

Why shouldn't they? Kabbalah works. When the wisdom and practical tools of Kabbalah are applied in life, positive experiences are the result. And Kabbalah can enhance the practice of any religion.

What Is The Kabbalah Centre®?

The Kabbalah Centre® is a spiritual organization dedicated to bringing the wisdom of Kabbalah to the world. The Centre itself has existed for more than 80 years, but its spiritual lineage extends back to Rav Isaac Luria in the 16th century and even further back to Rav Shimon bar Yochai, who revealed the principal text of Kabbalah, the Zohar, more than 2,000 years ago.

The Kabbalah Centre® was founded in 1922 by Rav Yehuda Ashlag, one of the greatest kabbalists of the 20th Century. When Rav Ashlag left this world, leadership of The Centre was taken on by Rav Yehuda Brandwein. Before his passing, Rav Brandwein designated Rav Berg as director of The Kabbalah Centre®. Now, for more than 30 years, The

Centre has been under the direction of Rav Berg, his wife Karen Berg, and their sons, Yehuda Berg and Michael Berg.

Although there are many scholarly studies of Kabbalah, The Kabbalah Centre® does not teach Kabbalah as an academic discipline but as a way of creating a better life. The mission of The Kabbalah Centre® is to make the practical tools and spiritual teachings of Kabbalah available and accessible to everyone regardless of religion, ethnicity, gender, or age.

The Kabbalah Centre® makes no promises. But if people are willing to work hard to grow and become actively sharing, caring, and tolerant human beings, Kabbalah teaches that they will then experience fulfillment and joy in a way previously unknown to them. This sense of fulfillment, however, comes gradually and is always the result of the student's spiritual work.

Our ultimate goal is for all humanity to gain the happiness and fulfillment that is our true destiny.

Kabbalah teaches its students to question and test everything they learn. One of the most important teachings of Kabbalah is that there is no coercion in spirituality.

What Does The Kabbalah Centre® Offer?

Local Kabbalah Centres around the world offer onsite lectures, classes, study groups, holiday celebrations and services, and a community of teachers and fellow students. To find a Centre near you, go to www.kabbalah.com.

For those of you unable to access a physical Kabbalah Centre due to the constraints of location or time, we have other ways to participate in The Kabbalah Centre® community.

At www.kabbalah.com, we feature online blogs, newsletters, weekly wisdom, a store, and much more.

It's a wonderful way to stay tuned in and in touch, and it gives you access to programs that will expand your mind and challenge you to continue your spiritual work.

Student Support

The Kabbalah Centre® empowers people to take responsibility for their own lives. It's about the teachings, not the teachers. But on your journey to personal growth, things can be unclear and sometimes rocky, so it is helpful to have a coach or teacher.

All Student Support instructors have studied Kabbalah under the direct supervision of Kabbalist Rav Berg, widely recognized as the preeminent kabbalist of our time.

We have also created opportunities for you to interact with other Student Support students through study groups, monthly connections, holiday retreats, and other events held around the country.

THE ZOHAR

Composed more than 2,000 years ago, the *Zohar* is a set of 23 books, a commentary on biblical and spiritual matters in the form of conversations among spiritual masters. But to describe the *Zohar* only in physical terms is greatly misleading. In truth, the *Zohar* is nothing less than a powerful tool for achieving the most important purposes of our lives. It was given to all humankind by the Creator to bring us protection, to connect us with the Creator's Light, and ultimately to fulfill our birthright of true spiritual transformation.

More than eighty years ago, when The Kabbalah Centre was founded, the *Zohar* had virtually disappeared from the world. Few people in the general population had ever heard of it. Whoever sought to read it—in any country, in any language, at any price—faced a long and futile search.

Today all this has changed. Through the work of The Kabbalah Centre and the editorial efforts of Michael Berg, the *Zohar* is now being brought to the world, not only in the original Aramaic language but also in English. The new English *Zohar* provides everything for connecting to this sacred text on all levels: the original Aramaic text for scanning; an English translation; and clear, concise commentary for study and learning.

THE LIVING KABBALAH
SYSTEM™: LEVELS 1 & 2

Take Your Life to the Next Level™ with this step-by-step, 23-day system for transforming your life and achieving lasting fulfillment.

Created by Yehuda Berg and based on his belief that Kabbalah should be lived, not merely studied, this revolutionary interactive system incorporates the latest learning strategies, addressing all three learning styles:

- Auditory (recorded audio sessions)

- Visual (workbook with written concepts and graphics)

- Tactile (written exercises, self-assessments, and physical tools)

The sturdy carrying case makes the system easy and convenient to use, in the car, at the gym, on a plane, wherever and whenever you choose. Learn from today's great Kabbalah leaders in an intimate, one-on-one learning atmosphere. You get practical, actionable tools and exercises to integrate the wisdom of Kabbalah into your daily life.

God Wears Lipstick: Kabbalah for Women
By Karen Berg

For thousands of years, women were banned from studying Kabbalah, the ancient source of wisdom that explains who we are and what our purpose is in this universe. Karen Berg changed that. She opened the doors of The Kabbalah Centre to all who would seek to learn.

In *God Wears Lipstick*, Karen Berg shares the wisdom of Kabbalah, especially as it affects you and your relationships. She reveals a woman's special place in the Universe and why women have a spiritual advantage over men. She explains how to find your soul mate and your purpose in life, and empowers you to become a better human being.

Also available: God Wears Lipstick Card Deck

I would like to dedicate this book to my beloved
grandmother, Esther, and my mother, Rachel,
who always taught me through their example how to
act with kindness, love, and compassion.

And to Karen, my spiritual mother who helped me
to be reborn. I thank you always, for showing us how to
see all the beauty of the world!

All my love,
Esther